Wisdom for Separated Parents

Wisdom for Separated Parents

Rearranging Around the Children to Keep Kinship Strong

Judy Osborne

PRAEGER

AN IMPRINT OF ABC-CLIO, LLC
Santa Barbara, California • Denver, Colorado • Oxford, England

Copyright 2011 by Judy Osborne

All rights reserved. No part of this publication may be reproduced, stored in a retrieval system, or transmitted, in any form or by any means, electronic, mechanical, photocopying, recording, or otherwise, except for the inclusion of brief quotations in a review, without prior permission in writing from the publisher.

Library of Congress Cataloging-in-Publication Data

Osborne, Judy.
   Wisdom for separated parents : rearranging around the children to keep kinship strong / Judy Osborne.
       p. cm.
   Includes bibliographical references and index.
   ISBN 978-0-313-39588-8 (hardback : alk. paper) — ISBN 978-0-313-39589-5 (ebook)
1. Separated parents—Family relationships.   2. Divorced parents—Family relationships.
3. Divorced parents—Family relationships—Case studies.   4. Divorced parents—Attitudes.
I. Title.
   HQ814.O788   2011
   306.874—dc22   2011008493

ISBN: 978-0-313-39588-8
EISBN: 978-0-313-39589-5

15   14   13   12   11   1   2   3   4   5

This book is also available on the World Wide Web as an eBook.
Visit www.abc-clio.com for details.

Praeger
An Imprint of ABC-CLIO, LLC
ABC-CLIO, LLC
130 Cremona Drive, P.O. Box 1911
Santa Barbara, California 93116-1911

This book is printed on acid-free paper ∞

Manufactured in the United States of America

Contents

Acknowledgments

Time to tell the story of this book.

I keep thinking of a book as a garden. You find a fertile spot and dig around, set some seeds, weed and tend, and only much later get to harvest some tomatoes or a rose.

It was after a presentation at an MIT seminar that I found the place for this garden. I have often presented seminars about divorce at the MIT Center for Work, Family, and Personal Life (codirected by Kathy Luneau Simons and A. Rae Simpson). At each seminar, people talked about the pains of separation. Would it last forever? It did not feel very helpful to say to people in pain "Things may be very different in three years." But Rae and I knew, from our personal and professional experience, that things *would* change. After one seminar, we wondered how we could tell the stories that we knew. And Rae said, "That's a book." And so the project began. I had found some fertile soil.

The interviews were the digging around. I am so grateful for all the people who were willing to tell me their stories, to go back into their histories and remember with me. Friends and colleagues and friends of friends. All were generous and interested and insightful about where they had been and how they made those transitions. And were ready to suggest the next person with an interesting story.

So I could begin the planting and, more importantly, the weeding. You will notice many names mentioned more than once. I am blessed by overlapping circles of friends and colleagues.

I shared the years from 2006 to the present with two groups focused on writing. Good friends and writers David Breakstone, Kathy Simons, and Rae Simpson shared life and love and wisdom in our twice-monthly meetings. They kept telling me to keep at it. Becky Sarah, Rae Simpson, Linda Varone, and I formed another group. They read endless drafts, encouraging me to "find my voice." Linda and I had extra breakfast meetings, shepherding each other's projects as we weeded.

Then I needed some thinning of the tender plants so that the strongest ideas might grow. My daughter, Emily Hanford, was a very early reader. She's a journalist, so I learned about her craft as she encouraged me. Emily helped me see the scope of the project, that these families were so common in her generation. Emily brought Sydney Lewis into my life. Sydney's professional editing experience and life with divorced parents helped shape many ideas in the book. I'm grateful to her for the notion that "our family forms outpace our language."

A writers' workshop with Susan Piver gave me a chance to read aloud to "strangers" and to feel their encouragement.

I have especially tender feelings about sharing the drafts of the introduction and my personal journey with my daughter, Emily Hanford, and my son, John Hanford, and his wife, Jacqui Hanford. I gave it to them and held my breath. It was very important for me to share it with them and generous of them to agree to read it. I still savor the sunset dinner I had with my son and my daughter-in-law as they so tenderly gave me their feedback and encouragement.

I had lots more weeding help from my college pals Elaine Elliot and Carol Kent. They were not only careful readers but provided much needed respite in adventures to movies, theater, and museums. Elaine was ever alert to verb tense and kept me supplied with tomatoes and eggplant from her well-tended garden.

A group of professional colleagues has listened intently and fondly to my life struggles as well as my professional dilemmas as we met for the past 20 years. Alan Albert, Laura Englander, Scott Reinhardt, and Judy Starr sat with me as I unfolded my ideas into this book. They, and Deb Clendaniel and Bob Read, also read carefully and pointed out weeds.

Four colleagues were helpful in giving feedback about the chapters on Untangling and Rearranging: Laura Englander, Geri Ferber, Kathy Simons, and Rae Simpson. Their wide-ranging personal and professional experiences gave my ideas much more clarity and breadth.

My son-in-law suggested his father, Maynard Goldman, when I needed to understand the legal aspects of book contracts.

Shaping the final version, like edging the garden, was done in collaboration with Susan Aiello, an enormously enthusiastic and competent editor.

So big thanks to all I can mention by name.

My clients cannot be named, but, over the years since 1980, I've learned about love and listening and waiting through transitions from their stories.

Mostly I learned to love by being a young mom to John and Emily all those many years ago. And there were lessons of love and loss as my children grew and I found ways to continue relationships with my stepdaughters, Sheila Boardman and Katherine Boardman. And then more transitions as I learned how to love my daughter-in-law, Jacqui Hanford, and my son-in-law, Derek Goldman.

Thanks go to my former partner, Sam Hanford, and his wife, Jane Hanford.

I want to dedicate this work to the spirited grandchildren in my circle of kin: Hannah and Rebecca Edwards, Chas and Oliver Goldman, and Robbie and Nevan Hanford.

I wonder what their grown-up families will look like. I hope that a more complex language and understanding about becoming parents will help future parents whether they continue together or apart.

1

Introduction: The Secret Life of Separated Parents

> People think it's odd that we talk on the phone. He could always reminisce about the past or dream about the future. We could spend hours at that. We've known each other for 42 years. I mean, how many people do you know for that long? I'll never have 40 years with anyone else except a sibling. (married 1964, separated 1986, divorced 1990, interviewed 2007)

At first, most separating parents are looking for relief and some space to get on with their lives. It was true for Susan, quoted here. There were years of struggle as she tried to get her husband to be a more involved father with their children. After separation, there were years of struggle over money. When the divorce became final, in 1990, Susan would have found it hard to imagine these long phone conversations.

I am a separated parent, too, separated since 1975, and have known the sadness and anger that developed into a more benign and cordial friendliness. I have also been a family therapist since 1981. My personal and professional life has been lived through the great wave of separations and divorces.[1] This wave of divorces during the late 20th century impacted our entire culture in one way or another.

In 1988, in the month that would have been my 25th wedding anniversary, I celebrated my daughter's graduation from high school, seated next to her father and his second wife of 10 years. In 2008, my former partner and I exchanged phone calls and e-mails arranging visitation again, this time for our grandson's visit during the month that would have been our 45th anniversary. We talk from time to time, and can reminisce about early days with respect and fondness for the history that we shared. We did not have to give up a part of that history out of anger and hurt.

I have seen these cordial connections repeated in the lives of many friends and know that most separated parents have ongoing connections. Some

connect around the rituals, holidays, and anniversaries of life and the accomplishments of their children. Some parents just show up to family events
and are casually interested in each other. Some parents stay quite involved,
with regular contact. Some separated parents have a great deal of contact
with each other when kids are young and then drift apart as children become adults. Like Susan, some parents have long, extended, and acrimonious
connections for years. They may soften back into a cordial space only after
grandchildren come along. Some separated parents add new partners to the
parenting unit and form new multiple-parent families.

I have often wondered when it is that separated parents realize that their
connection will be lifelong. It is not on their minds early in the process.

At first, separations are usually overly hostile or overly friendly. Neither
position holds for the long run. Initially, parents have jitters and anxieties as
they learn to be together again in public and in private. Some have new partners to add to the mix. But, as they meet for teacher conferences and graduations and school plays and baseball games and weddings, a benign energy
can grow to replace the old anger and hurt and sadness. They find new ways
of looking at each other—not just from the passage of time but from a mix of
events and experiences. These nuances can make for the messiness of life and
point to creative new family connections.

It is at moments of coming together in unconflicted ways that something
bigger starts to happen. As separated parents gather for celebrations, the benign energy can transform the old feelings. A new sense of relief and a change
in the expectations for family gatherings begin to grow. This new, less edgy,
and, perhaps, more positive tone can be powerfully healing for separated
adults and their children. To be in a room together in safety and comfort is
healing for the extended family, as well. Some separated parents and children
know this more benign energy early in their separation. Some learn this later,
when kids are well into their adult years. Much relief comes in learning to
feel comfortable together after years of custody battles, visitation changes,
and memories of lost trust. Parents can move from being adversaries to being
allies.

This is the secret. There is connection. It can be cordial.

Separated parents move through transitions with each other and with new
and former members of their extended families forever.[2] And not just because
of children. Sharing children is the impetus for most of the connection, but
they share a history long before children. Separated parents reminisce about
their early life together, their formative years of uncertainty, vulnerability,
and mistakes along their paths. Benign connections provide an opportunity
to understand the past as the next generation comes along. Grandchildren
make us kin in any case.

It is a secret in the larger society, as well. The big news stories are of anger
and alienation lingering between separated parents. Media may support anger
as the norm, because there are more dramatic feelings in the initial stages of

the formal separation. Drama gets attention. Researchers and journalists presume continuing struggle or chilly disconnection. A recent survey focused on the 35 percent of divorced couples who were not friendly with their former spouses and had contact only when necessary.[3] What about the other 65 percent? The experiences of the 65 percent who continue cordial connection, or come to cordial connection later in life, are underreported.

As Susan said, "People think it's odd that we talk on the phone." The media—and some professionals—have shaped that expectation and therefore leave parents, like Susan, feeling like outliers.

Just this summer, I was on a horse, on the top of a mountain in Montana, chatting with one of the ranch's wranglers. He asked about my book. I said it was about separated parents who found ways to stay connected. He stopped me very suddenly. He was excited to tell me about a couple with two children who had been guests at the ranch the prior week. "I saw how helpful the father was when the mom had trouble with her horse and said he'd likely get some good points with his wife for being so kind. The father looked surprised and told me they were not married and had been divorced for several years. They came to the ranch each year to continue a tradition for their daughters." Separated parents are everywhere, working to keep kinship for their children. Even on horseback, high up in a Rocky Mountain canyon.

THE INTERVIEWS

In my nearly 30 years of professional experience as a marriage and family therapist, I have heard countless family stories. I heard Susan's story. I heard stories of families like the one in Montana. Stories of respectful caring and shared pride in continuing to parent. Stories of an awareness of kinship.

Several years ago, I began to talk more formally about the long arc of history for separated parents. I chatted with anyone willing to share his or her story about ties to a former partner. Although they are well under the media's radar in our culture, I didn't have to work very hard to find these stories of connection.

Wisdom and sadness and joy emerged as these people talked about how they continued to be connected with a former partner in complex and serious ways. I began formal, taped interviews with an amazing group of more than 50 men and women. They had learned to look at endings without having to deny regrets and sadness. They felt that the feelings of sadness and regret helped to round out the edges of the old hurts and angers.

I decided to limit my interviews to people who had been separated for at least 10 years. After 10 years, most of the court-ordered connections about custody, visitation, and money are completed or are more or less routine. For the most part, the heat has been turned down on the power struggles. The legal ink has dried. By then, parents begin to feel free to participate in relationships with each other by choice and are often able to regain empathy and trust. When separated parents see that each is able to be devoted and constant for their children, much of the remaining hurt and anger and feelings of abandonment are held more gently. After a 10-year period, separated parents who have continued to care for their children see each other in softer ways—feeling respectful, albeit distant. Trust is more measured, more pragmatic, and more fragile.

Wisdom for Separated Parents is based on these more than 50 interviews with men and women from California to Maine, Wisconsin to Florida. They are nurses, professors, artists, therapists, lawyers, administrators of towns and universities, realtors, nonprofit consultants. Some are retired, some still working. All were married when their children were born. After separating, some parents remained single. Some went on to form gay and lesbian relationships and stepfamilies. Some went on to other heterosexual relationships, including a second marriage. Some parents were not yet divorced, although they had been separated more than 10 years.

For this book, the fact of divorce is irrelevant. The impact of separation—or separations—and what came after the formal separation is what shaped these families, the process of untangling and rearranging the physical, practical, emotional, and psychological aspects of family life while staying devoted to being parents.

WHAT'S NOT HERE

This is certainly not a definitive or comprehensive look at separated parents. The parents interviewed were largely white, middle-class North Americans. There were two mixed-race couples represented and numerous couples of mixed religious traditions. Those who volunteered to be interviewed certainly felt good about where they are today. They might tell a different story tomorrow or next year. We all see things differently from moment to moment. But these parents had reached a place of civility and pride in the growth of their postdivorce relationships. You won't find "toxic" relationships here.

And you won't find the children's voices here. Others have studied and collected the stories of the now adult children.[4,5,6,7] *Wisdom for Separated Parents* focuses on the adults and what happened for them. The adults made many transitions over the years as the legal and required connections faded. How they managed this is new territory. This is the secret that is underreported.

These stories begin to uncover the "secret" cordial ties. Telling the "secret" allows us all to have another lens through which to view the process of separation and divorce. We can start a conversation about how separated parents continue to care for their children. We can move from notions of "broken families" and "failed marriages" to remaking connections as successful separated parents. These parents wanted to talk about feeling successful and connected as they created lives apart while caring for their children.

LANGUAGE

When talking with separated parents, one always bumps up against the limits of the traditional language that the culture and media have used. Our family forms outpace our language. I recently interviewed a young woman, age 30, who told me of her parents' divorce when she was 14. In 2009, she said, "I feel embarrassed to tell you this, but my parents have a good relationship now. I don't know why but they do. It's kind of weird." I assured her that this was not uncommon. There are words that would better describe the realities of these families. A useful word is *kin*.

Kin

The possibility of using the word "kin" to describe separated parents emerged in the last 50 years.

In the mid-20th century, togetherness was the defining notion of family. Magazines and TV created the notion of perfect man-woman-two children families. Separations and divorces were alarming. When they occurred, parents were advised to make a complete split. A prominent professional journal of 1977 advised against parents' continuing involvement with each other. The report stated that parents who had "seemingly pleasurable post-divorce interactions were seen as suggesting an unconscious wish to 'hang on' to the marriage," which might be confusing and/or harmful to the children.[8]

Thank goodness that notion seems odd today. As separation became more and more common in the 1970s, parents began to demand shared custody.[9] Often perplexed and confused, professionals in schools and courts and mental health systems scrambled to understand how to support parents who wished to continue to share parenting responsibilities. For parents to remain closely connected and committed was the new adventure of the late 20th century. With joint custody legislation, first enacted in California in 1980, parents were pioneers in learning to live a family picture that was far different from what many could have imagined a decade earlier. They could think of themselves as close kin.

The word "kin" does give a definition to this web of continued family connection. A notion of kinship keeps children at the center, allows a parent to keep connections and to talk and think about success rather than failure. The extended family and friends can support a transition, not a division.[10]

"Kin" means connection through marriage. Legal action can sever marital bonds, but the ties through children remain. When there are grandchildren, being kin is a reality. Calling each other kin and using a language of change, acceptance, and commitment and devotion to childrearing allows us to expect and support these lifelong ties between separated parents.

The people who shared their stories with me struggled with language for themselves and their more complex and extended families. It is difficult to explain these continuing relationships without a change in language. I have purposefully not used the term "ex" except when quoting a parent. The point is that we don't have to think and speak in terms that suggest divisiveness. Extended family, friends, and new partners find it hard to understand attachments between former partners when negative language prevails.

Untangling

Another stumbling block is the language of separation. Any family that moves apart experiences the ending of a small civilization. Its history and customs must change. The conventional wisdom is that the change happens at the moment of public separation. But the people I talked to did not focus on the moment of separation or the day in divorce court.

They wanted me to understand the many smaller separations that led to a moment of formal separation or the moment of divorce. Marriages don't end in a big moment. Parents ended or changed their relationships in small ways. These people wanted to tell me how their marriages untangled over time. They could look back to see how things unfolded and how smaller moments of separation had shifted their ties to each other. They talked of silent debate within and then loud or sad talks with their partners. Even when marriages ended suddenly, these men and women spoke of the many signals and separations before one partner acted in ways that led to separation.

This is just what I wanted to understand, how the small differences and conflicts led to the decision to separate in a formal way and how that decision was experienced in the wave of divorces that swept these parents along. Some couples told of long years of struggle before the formal separation. Some couples were so stuck—like Velcro—that they needed hordes of professionals to untangle from each other. Some were determined to stay married and live separately to avoid legal intrusion in decisions about how to parent their children. As they told their stories, many understood their decisions in new ways. We learn as we tell our stories. We learn as we listen to stories.

Rearranging

Divorce is not only a single legal event but also a psychological chain of relocations, shifting relationships, and other changes. "Rearranging" is a more accurate word.

All families rearrange in large and small ways to accommodate growth and change. Rearranging around children happens all the time. Having children is the biggest change for any couple. Throughout history, fathers went to war and died. Mothers died in childbirth. Families rearrange as they include in-laws, grandchildren, and aging relatives. It is no different for parents who have separated. They simply rearrange at two different addresses.

Until the possibility of joint custody, there was no large sample that allowed us to see the variety of rearranging possible in families. Notions about "rearranging" are the heart of this book. There were no neat patterns in the rearranging of these families. But there were important factors that contributed to how they rearranged.

FACTORS IN REARRANGING

Five factors can shape the shifting connections between the former partners.

1. The most important factor is the ability of parents to shift from being former lovers to being co-parents. Letting go of old hurt, abandonment, and sadness is crucial. The couple must give up the struggle to renew adult intimacy and move forward, concentrating on co-parenting. The most important thing for parents to understand is that children need parents who are speaking respectfully to or about one another whether they are together or apart.

2. The ages of the children at the time of separation plays a part. Separating when children are young gives more time for finding a way to work as co-parents. There is more time for the energy between separating parents to become benign. People who "stayed together for the kids" reported long, energy-draining years of indecision. Those energy-draining years may have been as hard on children as any actual struggles about separation. Either way, there are costs—and benefits—for adults and kids.

3. Adult choices for a single life or a new partnership can also make for more or less connection between the separated parents. New three- or four-parent connections in stepfamilies enlarge the kinship circle. However, new partnerships can foster new struggles and family division. The struggles and family divisions can last for a while or forever.

4. Living near each other in the same community helps shape closer connections over the years but doesn't guarantee it. Some families rearrange across an ocean with great success.

5. Any life event or milestone has the potential to reshape relationships between separated parents. For example, children's illnesses or death in war bring parents into connection again. Events in the extended family, like funerals of former in-laws, do so, as well.

THE FUTURE FOR SEPARATED PARENTS— AN OXYMORON?

If you stay in touch with a former partner, connections keep changing. Wanting change or being pushed to change is what we humans do, individually or in relationships. Change is normal in families.

This is a secret, as well. Change is always possible for separated parents.

Decades after the children are grown and the legal ink has dried, issues continue to surface: Who has rights to retirement and Social Security benefits? How do I honor deaths of former in-laws? How do we share grief over our own or our children's illnesses? How can we share connection with common friends? Can there be talk of the shared history of the years before the separation/divorce?

Aging former partners may be drawn toward each other once again because our family circles get smaller in the upper register. As we live longer, we watch the fragility and death of former partners. We may find ourselves helping our children care for an aging parent, our former spouse.

And, with the passing of time, we may wish to connect over a current event. My former husband and I shared a Red Sox moment, in Kenmore Square, when "The Impossible Dream" team won and headed to the World Series in 1967. We remembered together in 2004. The death of Jerry Garcia brought two long-separated parents together for a good cry. Deadheads in their youth, who else would share that moment in 1995?

It feels strange to feel again the attachment to a former partner and difficult to explain to those who haven't experienced it. How do we deal with that with our kids, our new partners, our network of family and friends? Many of these family members and friends had feelings and opinions—and judgments— about the original separation. Those feelings and judgments may be just as strong when reconnections occur. Friends, who went through hell at the time of the separation and divorce, may be bewildered by this newfound openness to a civil connection and warm feelings. When warmth is reestablished, it is neither a threat to new partnerships nor an invitation to return to a daily kind of relationship. It may simply be a human response to an old connection and a long history.

No religious or cultural codes instruct former partners to honor and cherish each other or offer rituals and customs to follow.[11] How do you say goodbye when a former partner dies? Jackie said,

> I've always kept an eye on my sky miles. I have to save 25,000 miles so I can go to Dave's funeral. I don't expect him to live too much longer. He's frail. (married 1954, separated 1979, divorced 1982, interviewed 2007)

Who will get mentioned in obituaries? Were burial plots bought during the time together? Separated parents have lots of opportunities to live within the shadow of each other, tied in sticky and silly and serious ways for the rest of their lives. The relationships are more measured but always have the possibility of bumping against the borders of former intimacy.

PHOTOGRAPHS

During the interviews, I was shown many wonderful photographs. There were photos of recent holiday gatherings, of weddings, or of celebrations of grandchildren. Separated parents, their new partners, adult children with partners, grandchildren, and former in-laws—endless family connections. Those photos looked like a 1950s photo of extended family, but very few of our grandparents would understand the curious, tentative, and devoted connections that are very much alive and represented in these new photographs.

> This photo is our first Thanksgiving together with the kids since we separated 15 years ago. Even though she wanted the divorce, she didn't like to be reminded that I had a new relationship. The picture happened because she remarried and had her own new connection. Only then could she have us all together. That Thanksgiving was one of the best days of my life. I played music. My ex found the book of Beatles songs that I had given her on our honeymoon. I was surprised that she'd kept it all these years. I thought that was kind of nice.
>
> I'm curious to see what will happen when we get to the grandchildren level. It would be nice to have everyone come to one place. I hope we do it again. (married 1978, separated 1988, divorced 1996, interviewed 2008)

The gathering of family fed something deep in this man's soul. His new partner treasures the photo, as well. She says, "I was happy that it wasn't awkward anymore."

Photographs can have deep meanings. They made visible the reconnections and repair that had been possible in these families. The photos are tangible proof, reminding everyone that there are continuing connections after many years apart.

These are the family pictures of today. These folks know the particulars, the emotional truths within the photo, and now show them with pride. These were the pioneers, folks just moving along through their daily lives— adults and now grown children—changing the idea of family. This is the new American family. These are the families that were created while people were wringing their hands about the impact of divorce on children. It is a kind of family that the vast majority of Americans either live in or know in their communities.

HOW CAN WE USE THESE STORIES?

These stories support no particular position in the controversies about family. But these stories help to explain our family changes. These stories make it clear that grandchildren really are connected to everyone. These stories and a new language will help us to understand and expand realistic choices for families in the future.

The secret is out. The stories offer a complex and ambiguous picture of what happened for some parents who were lined up in the statistics of family changes in the past 50 years. The statistics were endlessly broadcast. The predictions were dire. Research suggested continued conflict and unhappiness. Parents lost sleep as they feared the effects of their decision to separate. They did not know, then, that they would be a part of creating this new picture of family.

In my own experience, I had thought that my working to stay connected as parents would give my kids a better sense of family. I didn't realize that, as we kept those ties for the children, I was also keeping a sense of family for myself. I didn't have to lose a chunk of my history. The history didn't look "conventional," but it was still there to be savored, regretted, and enjoyed. Over the years, I didn't have to angrily slam a door on that history.

Today's struggling parents and the professional helpers working with the pain in families need to know these stories. Raising kids is hard. It may be the hardest job in the world, but raising kids and trying to stay in a relationship is even harder. And harder still is staying in a relationship spread over two households and over many years. It is no longer helpful to talk only of failure of marriage. We need to talk about how these adults feel successful as parents.

Wisdom for Separated Parents provides models and ideas to spur creativity in shaping kinship circles around children. Divorce does not have to be unhappily ever after. I hope to challenge the language and the stereotypes around separation and divorce. Reviving the notion of kin can offer a new landscape for families. There are overarching themes here. In my experience as a therapist, I see these themes present in most couple relationships today. Society has changed its notions about family, but parents still struggle and stumble along with these challenges. The stories affirm the pioneering life decisions that many separated parents made during the past 50 years. And the decisions that some parents are struggling with today.

2

A Story of Untangling with Young Children in the '70s

> I didn't plan to separate or to become a statistic. I didn't plan for my children to become "children of divorce."

I'm sure most separated parents would recognize these sentiments. Marriages come together and apart in dances of intimacy and distance, adults weaving together and apart in many small ways. It is the hardest job in the world to learn to be parents together and to keep the adult partnership lively, to have differences and to stay connected. There is so much to know. It is very hard to pinpoint just what keeps a relationship alive and lubricated after a couple become parents.

My young husband and I were pals, and then we had babies. I wanted to be a good mom and not have the family of my own childhood history. I had no models for this hazy goal. When I separated, in 1975, I was not separating to get away from my husband. I wanted to be a good parent. Our struggles as a couple kept squeezing out more and more of the space to be that good parent.

ONCE UPON A TIME

We met in 1961 on a blind date in the fall of my senior year in college. In those days, college girls were supposed to have a husband on the radar by graduation. The college newspaper had a weekly column announcing who was pinned and who was engaged. It was that focused. As a straight, white, middle-class, college-educated girl, I expected to work but then to join a world of wives and stay-at-home mothers. Even though the Freedom Marches and the Peace Corps were on offer in 1962, nothing felt jarring about wanting to be a wife and a mother.

While I was growing up, in the 1950s, our culture did not give a very realistic picture of what being a wife and mother was like. *Father Knows Best* was the powerful image of family, and that picture certainly didn't jibe with my family.[1] The family I lived in included alcohol and depression, a combination that wasn't portrayed on TV, and didn't provide a very sturdy model for marriage and family. Although charming and competent at work and with friends, my parents were distracted and angry at home. Kids took care of themselves and fought to get attention. There was little space to escape from the family unhappiness. We were all alone, together.

Somehow I knew there was more. In college, I found courses in child development. A whole new world opened. I began to get an idea about what children really needed from their parents and how families might work.

So when I had my blind date as a college senior, I was ready to welcome a nice guy. He was funny and smart and serious. Not knowing his family or much about his background, I nevertheless sensed I could join forces with him and find my way into a new kind of life. He had finished college and was about to enter the navy. Those were the years of the draft and the lead-up to Vietnam. Being a naval officer fit with his family's profile. After training, he was stationed in San Diego to continue his life adventure.

I had been thinking about graduate school in child development, and finding a good graduate program on the West Coast was easy. I boarded a jet for LA to begin my own adventure—and to see what might develop between us. Jet travel was an adventure in itself in 1962. It was new. We dressed up for those trips. I wore a hat and gloves.

Those were playful days as we got to know each other. I was teaching in a nursery school in Pasadena. I bought an old 1954 Plymouth and each weekend drove the San Diego freeway, listening to jazz and smelling the orange blossoms from the groves that stretched down the coast from LA. Our relationship deepened in the California sun, and we told our families that we planned to marry.

And we did, in June 1963. I got a job teaching first grade in San Diego County, and he continued to serve on a small navy ship. We had more than enough resources and time to travel with friends and to explore how we were together. We learned to play and make love and manage bills and feed ourselves and change the oil in the car. We were becoming a couple.

By 1965, he was discharged from the navy, and we had a whole new set of choices. We could go anywhere, look for interesting work, and maybe start a family.

We had been able to save my salary as a teacher ($500 a month—a great wage in 1964), while living on his military pay. He wanted to become a teacher, and I wanted to study more child development, so our next adventure would be graduate school together. Children later. But, thinking about children made us want to be nearer to our families. Sunny California had been the place for exploration and some much needed breathing room for me—far from family and familiar landscapes. Now it made sense to head back to the East Coast, to family, to our familiar ocean and heavier weather.

We bumped along in our used station wagon across the country and landed in New York City for our year of study. Living in student housing, we spent every extra penny on theater tickets and music. We soaked in all the fall colors and the changing weather in New England. It was easy to be a couple. We had shared interests and similar pursuits, writing papers and doing internships, the stuff of graduate school.

We headed to new jobs in Boston after graduation, in 1966. He taught high school, and I worked as an elementary school guidance counselor. That was a new position in 1966 and gave me more opportunity to watch real parents and families. I was searching for models.

It was easy to make decisions together in those days, and we made a big one in 1967. Since we loved northern New England, we decided that we had enough money to buy a small house in the country, even before we owned anything in the city. As we worked to fix up that old country house, we began to know that we were ready to have a baby. We wanted to add the conventional roles of mother and father to our playful, adventurous connection as a young couple. So far, all our plans had worked out well.

BUMPS THAT SEPARATE

We hit infertility. After months of trying to conceive, doctors began tests. Lots of tests. No definitive reasons. What we wanted, we couldn't get. Sadness and anger and disappointment crept in. And our playful, fun-filled connection became a lot heavier. Why was this happening? What was wrong with me? Was I good enough? Was he good enough? What was wrong with us? Each month I felt more and more separated from him. Menstrual blood flowed and was devastating, announcing failure again.

I just didn't know how to handle that kind of disappointment or anger or grief. I cried alone and with him. He tried to comfort me. I didn't know how to talk about what I was feeling. We were stopped in our tracks. We didn't know how to be sad—alone or together.

My doctor suggested individual therapy. But therapy wasn't especially helpful in 1968 for this kind of family trouble. At that time, the Freudian model prevailed, with much of therapy focused on major mental illnesses. Group therapy and couple and family therapy were in their infancy. Most therapists were white male psychiatrists in suits behind desks. I went to therapy every week but couldn't find the words to talk about infertility or the sadness. But I did begin to understand about my own family, about what I had learned as a kid and what I might have to relearn to be a mother. In my Irish-English family, I learned little about talking and feelings. There were always a lot of words—and strong feelings—flowing around. But there was no resolution of the strong and conflicted feelings. Alone together, we didn't know how to connect about joy or sadness, to grow from life's bumps. I had no models to deal with the sadness and anger or to feel connected with my partner in sadness.

Nothing was moving in the fertility studies. All but one of the fertility tests was done on me. I felt even more separate. The use of fertility drugs and procedures were essentially unknown in the late 1960s, so we were spared the stress of drugs and invasive procedures that many couples face today. With each test, no definitive answers, just more uncertainty. And I felt damaged.

I just wanted a conventional life. I just wanted to have children. Infertility was the first thing in my adult life that I couldn't "fix." I couldn't just work harder. I had to face and accept this roadblock.

CONSIDERING ADOPTION

Gradually, the doctors began to introduce adoption as a way to make our family. We both wanted children, and in 1969 lots of couples were adopting. Cross-racial adoption was a new option that we considered.

It was a relief to make an appointment at the adoption agency. Now we could move ahead. Finally, we were talking together again, about being parents together. I no longer felt like "the problem."

The adoption process was amazingly helpful. "Why do you want a child?" The tears flowed for me as a simple clarity emerged, "I just want a baby. I want to be a mother." And the adoption social worker seemed to understand that perfectly.

We scheduled home visits and told family and friends. Then, to our great joy, we found we were pregnant. We were ecstatic. Our baby daughter was born in 1970.

As we settled into our nest, the baby brought new questions about love and devotion and what it meant to cherish and be cherished. What did it mean to be devoted for the long haul? To our baby? To each other? I began to understand I had a lot to learn about being a parent. Could we learn to be parents together?

ANOTHER SEPARATION

Sitting and rocking my baby in the quiet morning, feeling for the first tooth, feeling her fragileness, I awakened to something deep in myself. I realized that so much had been missing for me as a child. What I'd learned about children as a teacher didn't help. I didn't have any textbook baby here. I had a real, live child who needed me to be a grown-up. I began to know something deep about moms and babies and love. My heart opened, and I wanted to swim around in this new and mysterious emotional pool.

I recognized new yearnings in me, too. I wanted to cherish this baby and protect her. And I wanted to be cherished and protected. Being a pal didn't feel like enough anymore. I wanted to love this baby with him. I wanted that to feel equal. I kept noticing that he didn't seem to love the baby or me in the same ways. The differences led to a deep sense of separation from my partner.

With some big consequences, I began to think that I was the better parent. It is with some humbleness and embarrassment that I look at that now. What I knew intellectually about parenting began to come out as critical oversight of my partner. Underneath was my own sense of insecurity and anxiety about being a parent and a partner. I had grown up in a culture that gave most of the responsibility for home and hearth to the woman, so I was flooded with images of having the "perfect marriage and family." Such a big job. I projected my own insecurity and anxiety onto him, and it came out as criticism. I did not want to repeat my own growing-up family, which was far from perfect. But I was. I was repeating that critical, angry, disrespectful pattern that had been so much a part of my parents' marriage. I began to crowd his space as he tried to find his own way in becoming a father and a different partner. The criticism made him retreat. He had no models for hands-on fathering and no space from me to learn it. We both conspired to think I knew best. I encroached. He withdrew.

So we struggled along being happy and delighted with our baby and critical and angry and hurt by each other. We were withdrawing from each other, sharing fewer and fewer moments of connection and ease.

Not until years later did I understand deeply that becoming a parent always brings these kinds of differences to the surface. I didn't know then that parents could be very different and still connected.

WHO WORKS

When our little one was two, we faced another challenge to our notion of what it meant to be partners and parents. My husband lost his job. It was 1972. For a variety of reasons, we were able to see the job loss as an opportunity. The culture was full of talk about changing traditional roles. Ms. magazine had just been published.[2] Groups of women in the neighborhood were gathering. My mother's playgroup was becoming a consciousness-raising group.[3] It was not a huge leap for us to begin to discuss changing childcare decisions. Would I return to work? Would he take on major childcare responsibilities? Could I see myself as the one who made the money?

It was a fascinating set of questions, and a new world opened. I was intrigued about what it meant to be in the world of work and money. Only in the early 1970s were women able to apply for independent access to credit.[3] Before that, a husband or father had to cosign for loans and credit cards. I had been told by my father that I would be taken care of by a man and so didn't have to "worry my pretty head about money." It was a fairly common piece of advice to women in my generation. To be thinking about money—the topic that I thought was off limits—was very heady stuff. I asserted my equality in the marriage and said no to the old family ways all at the same time.

And my husband was delighted. He had been in business school before the navy. My interest in money and economics was a connection, something that joined us. Sorting out the questions of who would work and how we'd plan about money led to a deepening of how to be together as a couple. We became more equal in terms of money, in mapping out a financial future. This marriage was very different from our parents' marriages. We were learning to talk and to be realistic. After lots of exploring, we did come full circle, deciding that returning to the conventional roles of mom and dad was best for us. I really wanted to find out more about being a full-time mom. And he really didn't want to step too far out of the traditional male role. He would look for another job, and I would stay home.

That six-month period was wonderful for us. We were partners again. We were a part of the larger culture's questioning of the role of women and men and money and time. And my husband got to be at home with his daughter. He did the playgroup and took her to the park and made cheese sandwiches for lunch and was able to go to doctor's appointments and really get a taste of being a full-time parent. I was happy that we could change and work to change together.

FAMILY

As we went back to our differing roles, we were surprised and delighted with another pregnancy. We had none of the angst of fertility this time, and in 1973 our wonderful baby boy was born. They say that the second baby makes the family. And so we were: a mother and a father and a daughter and a son and some cats.

But having a second baby meant that the daily business of life separated us even more—he in the world of work away from home and me with the work of childcare in the neighborhood with other women and children.

I was not isolated. There was a "village." As a couple, we spent time with other young families and were especially close to two of those families. We three couples had wine in the late afternoons as children flowed around and husbands came back from work. We had suppers together and baths for kids and then home to bed.

We women became sisters and really blossomed as young mothers, learning from one another. We knew that women's roles in society were changing as we grew with our children. We'd gather in backyards and inhale Ms. I didn't feel trapped like the women of the 1950s. Then, all the yearnings had yet to be named.[4] By the '70s, language for women's changing roles was in the media and everywhere in our culture. We could feel safe imagining exciting changes ahead. And we didn't have to go out and do any of it. Yet.

As a couple, we had fun socially and loved our kids together and found intellectual ideas to engage us. But, for me, there was still a lot missing. Being a grown-up couple became more important to me. I was sensing how there could be more in intimate and sexual connection. Socializing with other couples and watching their closeness made me aware of my yearnings. Sexual questions were everywhere. We had just come through the years of "sexual revolution of the '60s."

These yearnings to be loved differently also led me back to criticizing his parenting. My uneasiness and yearning in the marriage found an easy target. Having found such a deep and loving way to be with our children, I wanted him to have that, too. I was picking on him, trying to get him to do it my way, and I didn't know how to stop. He was different and loving in his way. And that's really what kids need—two parents who love them in different ways. But I didn't let myself believe that he would find his own way. I didn't have a clue about how to change myself or to allow my husband to just be who he was. So I tried to change him. His picture of marriage and parenting was fuzzy, so he could not push back from a place of sturdy ideas and wishes about marriage and parenting. I needed a partner but didn't know how to be a partner. He retreated from the process of being thoughtful and courageous about change. I knew something was missing. I didn't know how to name that. Conflicts were filling up all the space and time.

ANOTHER LOSS

Another emotional blow came the year after the birth of our second child. In 1974, we found we were pregnant again. I was beside myself worrying whether I could still be a good mom to our new son and our four-year-old daughter. And we were both angry and sad that we might face an abortion decision after all the years of infertility. We struggled and cried on a camping trip and through a desperate weekend at a fancy resort. We sat on a beautiful porch, stunned and crying. I knew we were changing things with our decision to have the abortion.

But, with this decision, there was also great tenderness. We were being realistic and honest with each other. Making that decision—to have the abortion—we were together again. That made all the other things even sadder. Being connected and sad together was new for us.

After weeks of agony, we set an August date with our doctor and went to his office. We were very fortunate that abortion had become legal in the previous year.[3] I can't imagine the torture for couples who had to struggle with that important decision and had to take that action against the legal system.

The abortion decision and the anger, sadness, and grief were just too much for the unsturdy container of our adult relationship. To have moved through the infertility studies and the adoption interviews and then the joys of our two babies and now to have to make a decision about abortion was just too much. Too much to grieve. After the abortion, I was overcome by wave after wave of powerful feelings. I felt depleted.

Our little house in the country became a haven from all the conflict and struggle and strong feelings. There, we could relax and simply be together as a family. In the fall, we always closed the house for the winter. So, three months after the abortion, in October 1974, we were ready to close up again. I remember the day vividly. We had drained the water and shuttered up the house and were ready to leave. As I pulled the kitchen door closed, I knew for certain that everything would be different when we returned in the spring. I didn't know the shape of the change, but I was sure that change was coming.

All winter and deep into 1975, we struggled with the grief of the abortion. Finally, we began to ask whether we could go forward together. Night after night, once the kids were in bed, we sat at the kitchen table and wondered what to do. The table was round, made of butcher block, with a coating that could be scraped off by a fingernail. I remember relentlessly scratching that coating until the butcher block was fully exposed. Each scratch was another question with no good answer. To stay together or separate for a while? Could we decide together, or would one of us act or walk away?

THE DECISION

I walked one snowy afternoon that winter. It was dusk, and all the lights made our two-family houses and the nearby Victorians cozy and inviting. Sturdy pine trees were covered with snow, and the windows were sparkling with light. My house sparkled, too—from the outside. But I knew what roiled behind that sparkle. I knew of the troubles in those other houses, as well as the trouble in my house. I had learned to allow sadness in. And there was a kind of peace in knowing about the sadnesses of life, as well as the joys. Sadness can be as peaceful as the falling snow.

One couple in our neighborhood had separated. And had come back together again. They had worked hard and seemed to have learned a lot from separating for a while. We thought that separating temporarily might help us. We didn't know it then, but we were smack in the gathering cultural wave of divorces in the '70s and early '80s.[3]

We kept on talking and doing the laundry and taking the kids to the park and making plans for summer vacation. Then, one day, a seemingly small argument about money erupted into the final moment for me. Action and anger were always lingering in the wings. Often, a single moment of anger organizes long months or years of talk into action. Anger can erupt into the "that's it" moment. I went from having questions to having clarity.

In our earlier struggles about who would work and who would do child-care, we had promised to talk before acting on any big purchases. One day, he announced a big purchase. He had spent a lot of money before we talked together. I didn't want to say no to things, but I was working hard to keep promises, and with this I felt slapped. I'd been working so hard to do things together, to make decisions together. In that moment, my trust was eroded. My spirit of cooperation just evaporated. I felt angry but didn't want to struggle and fight anymore. I went from fearing separation to seeing it as the only choice—a break in the relentless sapping of energy for both of us.

The big expenditure was for ski equipment. It was not an expenditure for the family or for us as a couple. Those skis represented something intolerable in the moment. He was skiing off into his own space. The trust was gone, and I felt alone. That was my "that's it" moment. Others have those moments when learning about an affair or having one too many arguments or one too many moments of alcohol or drug use. The "that's it" moment organizes the months or years of talk into action. Things achieve a certain clarity, a certain focus.

Instead of being able, or wanting, to learn more about the ambiguity and complexity of these moments, I moved to separation as a way to resolution. I was done.

That night, I said the words, "I want a separation." Later I stared out into the trees surrounding our second-floor apartment, looking into the dark night, not knowing who I was or what all of this was about. Why make such a big deal about a pair of skis?

And, after those words were spoken, our small civilization was changed forever.

In a few days, in our lime-green, orange, and yellow 1970s living room, we told our children, then two and five. "Daddy is going to have a new place to live. We love you very much, but we don't want to fight so much." Our carefully rehearsed words and the unscripted tears said much to those sad and bewildered faces. I remember that both of them ran away. Then there were hugs. Then awkwardness. Then numbness. Then proceeding with the needs of little kids—dinner, baths, diapers. The physical and scheduling demands of young kids are soothing and, for parents, can balance overwhelming feelings.

LOOKING BACK

My story of separation has many parts that will feel familiar to couples who have lived that kind of middle-class life. In my experience as a therapist, there are overarching themes here. It is a story of weaving in and out of separation and connection. While the separation seemed sudden to those outside, our marriage had been oozing apart over many years even as the weaving in and out continued. We felt separated through infertility and close through abortion. We wanted to be parents and didn't realize how becoming parents makes for both powerful closeness and powerful separation. We felt separated by cultural expectations and family notions of gender roles. And we also felt connected to each other through cultural changes and choices about male and female roles. At times we worked to connect through the economics of family life, and then we separated over the reality of one money issue.

And, for us, the grief was too much. Walking though choices about infertility, adoption, pregnancy, abortion, and eroded trust was just too much weight for our marriage.

Although I had been so critical of his parenting, it had never been a question of his not being a father to our kids. There was never any doubt that we would go forward as parents. It was all about separating as adults—we needed more space to become parents in our own ways. And we needed some peace from the conflicts woven in and out of our adult relationship. We were making a decision to separate. Our neighbors had shown us it could be safe to separate for a while. They separated and found a way to recommit to being a couple again. We did not know our separation as partners would be permanent. We did not separate in order to divorce.

What we didn't know then was how much our lives would be connected forever. We'd have to figure out so many things, whether we were together or apart. It is not the commitment that the two adults make to each other. It is not the marriage. It is the fact of having children that firmly establishes kinship. The question of separation highlights that the kinship is forever. The critical thing is how parents work with the kinship over the years. Some parents are unable to accept thinking about being tied forever. Some parents just vanish or make an appearance once in a blue moon.

We were committed to not disappearing from each other's lives. And that is what this book is about—not disappearing.

OTHER STORIES

This is my story of family. My former partner has another version. We know only our own stories and have to be mindful of that always. All couples have at least two versions of their life together, one for each of them.

I was privileged to hear many stories for this book. Listening to the stories of other couples helped me identify some patterns in the ways parents separate. I'll leave my story here and go to those patterns and to other rich and varied family stories.

Untangling: Normal Differences and Formal Separations

All parents experience normal separations as they bring their baby home. They are no longer lovers and pals imagining a family. They are living a family.

My story was surely that. We experienced the separateness of gender differences as we faced the facts and the feelings about fertility. After our child was born, we passed through a door into the world of parenthood. My daily life was shaped by childcare work at home. My husband's daily life was shaped by work in the community. Becoming a parent changed the focus of our time together and our time apart. Each of us learned to see ourselves as parents from a different platform.

NORMAL DIFFERENCES BETWEEN PARENTS

As we hold our first child, most of us feel deeply connected to each other and to the baby. And then the changes begin. The first baby, whether in a first family or in a new stepfamily, brings a profound shift in the relationship between the two partners. The need for connection and attachments shifts. Partners now look at each other as parents.

Elena and her husband met in Europe and moved to the United States to continue their work, she in social science research and he in the art world. They began their relationship with an understanding of sexual openness. Their open relationship worked well. They respected each other's work and the search for truth in the world of science and art. They loved their differences and respected their explorations, sexually and intellectually. And then they had a baby. Becoming a mother immediately changed Elena's personal goals.

> Standards for commitment and marriage were different for each of us. That was fine at the beginning. I wanted more of an open relationship

at first. But that changed as soon as I had my child. I needed something more committed. I wasn't willing to live that way anymore. I needed family. I needed more security. I needed more commitment from him than he was willing to give. I wasn't thinking about separating, but I wanted more.

Caring for a baby brings us up against many differences. There are aspects we can know about our partners before making a commitment, but knowing how the person will be as a parent is usually not one of them. We may watch our partner interacting with children and see a wonderfully playful man or woman. But that does not predict how he will be when caring for a child all day long or reacting to a crying infant in the wee hours of the morning.

It was red flags the first week we brought our daughter home. Right away, we had arguments about parenting. She would cry. I would go to pick her up, and he would tell me not to. He thought she should just scream. I would yell and say, "No, my baby's crying. I'm going to pick her up and cuddle her." He'd say, "Well, the books say you should let her scream, and that's how we should be raising her. We've got to let her tough it out."

In addition to differing ideas about what babies need, there begins a division of time and energy in caring for children on a daily basis. No matter how equal the partnership before the baby, things change. How each parent spends time and energy becomes, in big and little ways, quite different. Most cultures divide the worries and concerns of child care *unequally*, regardless of whether the parents are gay or straight. One parent takes on or "gets" the primary job of juggling caregiving responsibilities with whatever else is on that parent's plate. Caregiving activity and emotional involvement become unequal. This is often unanticipated by either parent.

We didn't know how to do all the family stuff. I felt I had way too much responsibility. There were years that he was getting up and leaving before the children were even up. It wasn't his fault. It was just the job he had. I didn't want to move, so he had a very long commute. That did a lot of damage to the relationship. I was just overloaded, doing all the child stuff and the financial stuff. He was definitely involved with our kids, but I just got overwhelmed by feeling I had to do everything. If we'd been more sophisticated about marriage and families and what's involved, we might have worked it out. No one sat me down to say what was involved in having kids, and I didn't have any psychological training to prepare me.

This is a perfect description of what happens for many couples. Without a lot of deep discussion or serious thought, the tasks get divvied up, patterns are established, and life moves along. Helping young families normalize these differences is important. There are no Hallmark cards to highlight these difficult and shaping decisions in how to care for children and how the caregiving becomes unequal. Helping new first families and new stepfamilies navigate these transitions can do much to prevent the resentment and isolation that many parents feel when the roles of caregiving pull them in different directions.

Rethinking the roles of mother and father was a big public dialog in the '70s and '80s as women began to move into the workforce and to rethink their notions of housekeeping and childcare.[1] Gloria, married in 1970, reflects this.

> There were a lot of strains. We didn't have lots of money. He was in grad school. I was struggling with having dropped out of grad school and feeling like a failure. So I became the breadwinner. He started a part-time job and did a lot of the childcare, more than I did during the week. On the weekends, I did most of the childcare. Part of the woman's movement was the tough stance about childcare and housework. I would rant: "We have a kid, and you will do 50 percent of the childcare! I'm not doing it all and cooking and all kinds of housework!" I was adamant. I did not want to be a homemaker.

Another aspect of normal differences between parents is how we behave as parents as the children grow. Who comforts children? Who's in charge of baths and bedtime? Who makes medical appointments? Who cooks for kids? Who cooks for the adults? How do you play with a kid? Who disciplines? Who coordinates homework? Some parents find it easy to cope with these differences. Some find deep places of contention. Most parents think they are "right." And they do not want to notice that the other parent has another version of "right."

Partners consider themselves to be right because each brings a different imprint from his or her own family of origin about what it means to be a parent. Most of us are not very conscious of the strong patterns that we bring from our growing-up families. We learn most about parenting when we are very little. We think it's just "the way you do it." Unless we make a conscious effort, we tend to repeat patterns from our own childhood, from our own family culture.[2]

And many of us don't know how to talk about these differences. Our culture hasn't done a very good job helping parents *learn* to be parents. We just assume we know how to do it. Because the ways of caregiving and being married are so unconscious, we simply juggle and struggle. No one sits us down and teaches us how to shift into being a parent, shift into being a family.

When we were little, we learned by example. We watched and learned about family. Without words.

And, without words, we are not able to have a dialogue about our differences or even to reflect on what we've learned. If family backgrounds are similar, conflicts are fewer. But no two families are completely alike.

Nan and her husband married in 1970 and, as a young couple, were active politically and socially. They headed up fundraising for a large, urban arts organization. They had similar energy levels and loved connecting with other energetic couples. However, they had very different experiences of growing up. As a child, Nan had lost a parent and had felt adrift without family connection and without many financial resources. Her husband was from a large extended family, wealthy and socially active in the community. His family was primarily focused on adult connections. Their differences emerged as the babies were born.

> We were very social in that first six years before we had babies. Then my connection to the baby became really kind of magical. I wanted to bring my husband into that connection, but he really wanted to continue our busy social life. His mother and his grandmother were wonderful hostesses. It was exhausting—all these big parties. I just couldn't breathe. I think I had a mini panic attack when I realized how suffocated I was starting to feel.

Nan had found adult social life thrilling at first and had wanted to enter into the world of her husband's family. She did, and did the entertaining well. Then the baby came. All the early yearnings for family were suddenly present in a very profound way. She found life with a baby "magical." Her husband did not. He had not had losses that would make parenting "magical." It was not his family experience.

These unconscious and unexamined differences are normal and common for all parents. We all have the task of coming to terms with the models we bring from our families of origin. And the task of learning how to allow for our partner's different parenting style. That is what makes having children such a busy adventure. We all have an opportunity to see our own families in a new light and to sort out what we want to keep and what we want to learn to do differently.

So, while all this difference is normal, it is unsettling for parents. The job of being a good enough parent and keeping an adult love relationship alive is really tough.

UNTANGLING: MOVING BEYOND NORMAL DIFFERENCES TO FORMAL SEPARATION

In the interviews, the number one topic of conversation was how each partner felt like a successful parent. Some felt they had worked in a good parenting partnership right from the beginning of their separation. Some felt successful only on the long look back over the lives they had led apart as they cared for their children.

A second important topic for these parents was how they had moved apart, how their relationships had untangled. They wanted me to know how their marriages had changed before there was any formal separation. They wanted me to know that the decision to separate had not been whimsical or willfully mean. The decision had emerged from the struggles about how to be married and parent together. They wanted me to know their moments of connection and strength as a couple, too. They were insightful as they looked again at the moments of separation, the process of untangling. Most parents wished to be successful parents, even as their adult love relationship diminished.

> Once I actually went through the whole process of separating, I looked back on it and said: My marriage was not a failure. We had two beautiful children. We did all this great stuff and then we decided we needed to do something else, so we moved on. There was nothing failing about that. No, just because you get divorced does not mean you failed.

Formal separation goes beyond the normal differences into a new set of issues and concerns. It is useful and important to understand that all families have normal parenting differences and smaller normal separations. Knowing the normal differences helps to understand formal separation in a broader context.

THE PROCESS OF UNTANGLING TOWARD FORMAL SEPARATION

Marriages don't end in a moment. It is important to understand and appreciate this. These parents give us a gift by talking about the process. They walked me through their connections and separations. The process became clear as I listened.

1. First, it is a notion in one partner's mind. The notion of separation begins to take more and more shape as one person struggles with the idea: "If I separate, can I be emotionally and physically safe? What about the children?"
2. Second, that idea and the questions may be shared with the other parent or acted out in an affair.
3. Third, the idea is somehow shared with children and other family members and close friends who may witness the growing tensions. Loud arguments may flood family life.
4. Fourth, the decision to separate is shared publicly by making separate living arrangements. Friends, neighbors, and coworkers now know. Privacy is surrendered. "As soon as she moved out, the roof

came off our house and everyone thought they could see what was going on."

5. Finally, a legal step may be taken: formal separation or divorce.

The timetable of untangling is varied. Some partners moved through the process in months, whereas others, as you will see, took years.

PRIVATE THOUGHTS OF UNTANGLING

All the normal ways to feel different are the warp and woof of every family's struggle. But, out of those differences, some parents begin to contemplate formal separation. Thoughts of separation evolve. Usually, the notion rattles around in one partner's mind.

I got into therapy along the way in the marriage. I ended up feeling extremely alone. We spoke totally different languages, and we had a third language. In that language we could say, "Please pass the salt." I knew that the separation was coming for four or five years before it actually got there. So it was civil but extremely strained for all that time. (married 1975, separated 1993, divorced 1997, interviewed 2009)

The thought of wanting to separate rattled around for four or five years for Jan. She had no models for sorting out the tensions she was living with. Jan lived in a suburban community of conventional-seeming families. She remembers very little evidence of marital troubles around her. So, she lived with questions and the shame of having those private thoughts. She was afraid to take the roof off the house. Thank goodness, she was able to see some value in the experience of therapy and not be alone with all the tension and questions.

Another woman got her notion about the possibility of separating after a medical emergency.

I had a stroke in my 40s. It was a wonderful wake-up call. I decided I wanted to understand what had happened in my body by going back to school to learn body work. That's when I started doing all the personal growth work. I realized I was changing, and he just wasn't changing. His definition of a fine marriage and my definition of fine were quite different. (married 1966, separated 1995, divorced 1996, interviewed 2007)

It can be a medical emergency or simply reaching midlife that wakes us up to questions about what we want, about how our energy is being used. Often, when our children grow to adolescence, these questions come to the fore. As teens begin their own explorations of sexuality and life goals, we are often pushed to reevaluate our own choices and goals. This is one of the gifts of having teens. It makes for turmoil, but it is a gift.

SHARED THOUGHTS OF UNTANGLING

At some point, the private thoughts about separation are shared with a partner or acted out in an affair. Some couples begin by talking about others who are separating, friends or people in the media. They talk about separation in a hypothetical way. They are not ready to speak directly about their own wishes and fears.

> Two years before we separated, we went to a wedding and we talked hypothetically about separation. Later, we went on a long vacation, and I had a horrible time. When I got home, I knew that this was the end of the line. I was fed up and hurt and isolated. As we talked, it was clear that he figured lots of people aren't happily married and that was okay with him. His parents had a long, lonely marriage. I didn't agree with that at all. I thought that it was not a good model for the children. We finally got able to talk about what might happen. It was just hard to really look at where we were. (married 1975, separated 1985, divorced 1986, interviewed 2008)

Other couples use professional settings to begin the conversation. In a therapy or pastoral counseling setting, people are often able to speak more clearly and honestly. They usually hear more clearly, too.

> We were having problems, and we recognized it, and we really didn't want to split up. We had two very little children and were committed to the relationship. We went to therapy and that confirmed why we shouldn't be together even though we had little ones. Sitting and talking with each other let us realize that. And then there was one incident. We went to a party one night and he absolutely ignored me. Every time I walked into a room where he was, he would leave. When we got home that night I said, "It's over, I can't live this way. You were cruel." We were both crying. I said the words, but he knew. He kind of pushed me until I said the words. So I would finally say it's over. To me that's kind of classic. (married 1968, separated 1980, divorced 1981, interviewed 2008)

The talk is not always calm. Action and anger are always lingering in the wings. As this woman says, "then there was one incident." As in my own story, a single moment galvanized months of talk into action.

There is sometimes no direct talk about separation. One or both partners act by having an affair, either on an emotional or a physical level. An affair signals to one's self and one's partner that something about their adult love relationship is no longer enough.

> Life was unbearable together. We struggled. I had no idea what marriage involved. I never felt centered with one man. He was having affairs, and

I was, too. It wasn't my first affair by any means, but this one was big enough to have given me the thought that I could have something more in a relationship. I was pretty sure I couldn't have this with my husband. A good friend knew what I was doing and said, "You know what you are doing isn't good for you and it isn't good for him or the children." Nobody had ever said that to me. I thought about it, and it seemed right. Then I could think about the real issue, which was separation. (married 1964, separated 1976, divorced 1978, interviewed 2007)

This woman was very lucky to have such a friend, one who could help focus her attention on the consequences and meaning of her choice to have affairs. She could focus on finding a creative way through the troubled marriage. She and her husband both went on to long and solid committed relationships.

Sometimes the discovery of an affair is sudden and surprising.

I thought everything was going along well. We had two kids, two and four at this point. But, one summer on vacation, he was very depressed. When we got home, he said, "You know I don't have to stay married to you for the sake of the children." It came just like that. He began to be quite verbally abusive. Everything I did seemed to be wrong. Then, one day, I saw him getting ready to go on a trip. He had bought all new stuff. I began sneaking around. I put the pieces together and found out about the affair. Then all hell broke loose, and it was just horrible. He would leave at odd times and not be part of the family. When he would be there, we'd start fighting with each other. All the things you should not do in front of children. (married 1987, separated 1998, divorced 2000, interviewed 2009)

For some parents, there is no acting out in an affair, nor is there any direct discussion. They simply have in-house separations with separate sleeping arrangements, separate lives.

We were always very separated. We did not have a tight emotional connection ever. I knew before I got married that I was going to be lonely, going to be disconnected. The kids were in junior high. Therapy wasn't going anyplace. I had moved out of the bedroom while we were in couples therapy. No words were spoken. He acted like it never happened. For a long time, we shared a house and never saw each other because we kept different hours. He'd be downstairs, and I'd be upstairs. It was easy in a big house. I was staying for the kids. I thought that was the right thing to do. But when they went to college, it was unbearable. I began to think; I just can't be an authentic person and stay in this marriage. I just moved to an apartment. But we didn't divorce for another 13 years. (married 1969, separated 1996, divorced 2009, interviewed 2010)

This couple felt separated very early in their relationship but continued to live and look like the conventional definition of married. It took 40 years for them to make the moves that added them to the statistics for divorce. Their kids were never "children of divorce" in the way the media paints the picture. What do we call this family? We need to find ways to think about families that do not lump them into categories that are yes/no solely on the basis of a legal event.[3]

However each parent chooses to bring the question of separation to the table, one way or another the notion becomes part of a dialogue (perhaps a loud dialogue) between the partners. A long or short period of time follows in which the talk of separation is private, between the parents.

And when that privacy is surrendered—either by telling or by shouting—children and the extended family finally know what is happening. The roof does come off the house. The private boundaries of the family become public.

GOING PUBLIC AND LEGAL

The public disclosure of the separation comes when living arrangements change. Parenting continues in two spaces, and the neighborhood and the larger community are privy to the parental separation.

Divorce really tore the neighborhood apart as well as separating the families. In one family, the father left and the kids were either gone some of the time or all of the time. Those were my kids' friends. They weren't all here at the same time anymore. Family schedules weren't synchronized. This is an unexpected consequence of separation: the neighborhoods split up, not only the families. It was less of a neighborhood because of the divorces.

The whole world can then be witness to the untangling of a small civilization. Everyone in the family tries to find a way to explain. At first, most people blame someone or something. It's *his* fault or *her* fault, or, as some kids and adults say, "It's the divorce force."

It is only this final step that may take the whole family into the legal domain.

What we study and call parental separation and divorce is simply the public and legal arrangement that follows a sequence of untangling separations. Instead of simply looking at parents and children after the formal separation and divorce, the moment in time at divorce court, we need to expand our understandings of how each couple untangles and the impact of the untangling on adults and kids.

Divorce is blamed for family change, but, typically, divorce is simply one part in the experience of untangling. Divorce is *not the cause* of untangling.

FOUR PATTERNS OF UNTANGLING

As I heard these unique family stories, there were also commonalities. The commonalities pointed to four distinct patterns of untangling: sudden splits, oozing apart, stuck-like-Velcro, and separated/still married.

Sudden Splits

Some parents literally split apart like a rock hit by a sharp object. A sudden awareness of an affair or, perhaps a surprise discovery of heretofore hidden sexual identity, creates a dramatic moment of separation.

We separated only once. I basically fell in love with someone else. The whole thing was lightning fast. I first saw my present husband in October and went to meet his family in November, and I moved out in December. Three months, and I was in a different house. (married 1972, separated 1985, divorced 1988, interviewed 2007)

I found out he was gay. I found out by accident. I found this letter in his briefcase. It was a love letter from a man. I was looking for a map and I found it. I had to read it about 10 times as it sunk in. Everything changed in that moment. (married 1973, separated 1995, not yet divorced, interviewed 2008)

Oozing Apart

Some parents ooze apart, gradually and steadily, over time, with many small separations in the untangling process. First the internal dialogue that separates one from the original family commitment. Then the doubts and questions with your spouse. Maybe therapy. Maybe no more sex. Sleeping in another room. The family is crumbling, and no one can take the steps to make the repairs that are needed. By the time the decision to separate is announced, older kids might say, "What took you so long?"

A retired educator spoke about how his marriage oozed apart. He had married in 1961, at 30, and had three children in the first few years of marriage.

My story involves a spouse-swapping deal and six children who are all one big blended family now. We called it wife swapping then, and it was pretty common in the '70s in the academic, intellectual circles. We got to know this other couple in our church. The husband was getting into the sexual revolution literature.[4,5] They started courting us. It was a little alluring at first, and then, the next thing you know, we were making out with each other's wives. Probably within a year, we openly gave permission to each other to have sexual relations with the other partner.

We each had three children, all the same ages. All in elementary school. So for five years, the two families did family things together, too. We really enjoyed our children and the connection as families. Meals, church, summer trips.

And through it all, it was clear that the primary sexual partners had been exchanged, but my first wife and I continued to live together. We had a quasi in-house separation. We never got to a place of sleeping in different rooms, but my wife and I stopped having sex with each other.

Other parts of our marriage became more tenuous, so I started looking for a job in another part of the country. My wife and I wrestled with it and agreed that we needed to get out of town. We couldn't hold our relationship together for the kids if we didn't leave. I was brought up to think that divorce was out of the question, so we moved in 1975 to "save our marriage," and all that happened was that it got worse. The ties, the emotional ties with the other two, didn't wane. After about another year, with some therapy, we agreed that our marriage was gonzo, and we would go in the direction of separating and legally switching partners. I went back to my really core love. I called her and said, "I want to marry you. So, can you just come out here?" She had separated from her husband that year.

So in 1980, the great switch was made. My second wife moved in with me in January of that year. The divorce wasn't final, so my ex-wife had to stay in town for the court date and for the kids to finish school. There was six months overlapping time when both women were here in the same town. They had become very close friends, so there was no animosity. (married 1961, separated 1979, divorced 1980, interviewed 2007)

This marriage oozed apart over many years and many moves. The process wasn't stuck. It was planned. The adults struggled and kept boundaries in place. The two couples made space for the shift in adult partnerships, mindful of making space for children, too.

Oozing Sadness and Anger

Looking at your family life as it comes apart brings up a lot of sadness. Some separations ooze apart through such a long period of questioning that the sadness becomes unbearable. It is easier to feel angry. People have trouble understanding that sadness can make one very angry. "Better mad than sad" is a useful truism. So, after a long period of oozing apart, the break may be possible only in a moment of anger. The anger is surprising—and not so surprising.

We were in therapy off and on for 10 years. One day I had requested he move out briefly, because we'd had a big fight and I was scared. I asked him to just leave for a few days so things would calm down. That's when we finally separated. He just wasn't willing to try again. When we talked 10 years later, I asked, "Why did you leave?" and he said, "I didn't leave. You told me to leave." I said to him, "Well, I asked you to leave for three days and you left for a lifetime." (married 1965, separated 1987, divorced 1990, interviewed 2006)

To the outside world, this separation looked like one of the sudden-split separations. Actually the couple had inched along for 10 years, through many therapies, and then each took steps toward formal separation.

A final break may come when one partner suddenly recognizes the tensions that have been there for a very long time. This couple, a businessman and a stay-at-home mom, had been oozing apart until events pushed new understandings to the fore.

We weren't very happy for many years, but we had four little kids, so I didn't know I had any options. We were together until he had a panic attack and ended up in the hospital. He was diagnosed bipolar. The psychiatrist said to me, "I know what's going on here. This is classic bipolar." So I took a referral, and I had two therapy appointments. I told the therapist that I wanted to get out but was terrified to be on my own. She looked at me and said, "You are already on your own. You're doing it all anyway." When she said that, it gave me courage. Within a week or so, I talked to a friend about getting a lawyer. (married 1964, separated 1980, divorced 1981, interviewed 2007)

Stuck Like Velcro

Other parents are stuck like Velcro, so stuck together that hordes of expensive and caring people get involved. Therapists, clergy, accountants, friends, lawyers, and courts all contribute to the prying apart of the still-grasping parents before and after the date of the divorce. Most of the parental struggle is fueled by fear and anger. These are often the high-profile divorces in the media. These parents keep spinning and sliding on the ice with no traction to get out, no ways to emotionally separate from each other. They often have little energy for their kids or for new partners.

What a hot connection we had at first. But soon I was afraid of him. I didn't think of him as an alcoholic, but he drank a lot. He had guns and behaved threateningly. I was really afraid of what he might do. I just couldn't get out of that relationship.

At one point, he knew I was thinking about leaving. He had an agreement drawn up evicting me from my house and taking custody of our son. He never did anything with the papers, but I wasn't going to sit around and wait for him to change his mind. So I brought my son back to the East Coast. He followed, and we divorced.

He moved in with a woman who had children from a previous relationship. He started to ask for shared custody because his new wife had shared custody. I was worried about his drinking and the violence and wanted my son to be safe. We worked with a mediator and got an agreement. Then right before the hearing, he contacted the mediator and bullied him into changing everything in his favor. Going to the custody hearing was a total surprise to me. There was nothing presented that had been a part of our mediation. I was really just devastated, devastated. I couldn't believe it. And nobody stopped the bullying.

Everything changed again when he started to do family therapy with his new partner, her children, and our son. I was invited to participate and said yes for my son. In the therapy, it really started to become clear to me that my son was acting angrily in response to all this craziness that was going on between us. I gave up the fight because I could see that my son was carrying way too much tension. I gave up trying to have full custody. I just let it go. We ended up just doing what my ex wanted. For a while, we had shared custody. But he divorced that wife and stepfamily and quickly moved far away from his son again. So what was all the struggle about? I'm glad I found a way to let go. (married 1978, separated 1983, divorced 1985, final custody resolution 1989, interviewed 2006)

Lawyers, mediators, judges, therapists, family, and friends were involved in the untangling of these unhappy parents. Many years of exhausting struggle drained energy from everybody. Even a new marriage failed to make any separate emotional space for these two. These parents and their child entered the formal legal statistics in 1983, but it was not until 1989 that custody issues were untangled. The date of the divorce for these people was a brief moment in a long, long drama. The real untangling came after she recognized her son's tension and was able to let go of her part of the struggle.

Separated/Still Married

Some separated parents are not yet divorced after 15 years or more. For a variety of reasons, parents may choose to separate but not take formal legal action. Some choose to live apart but wait until children are of adult age to finalize the legal agreements. When children reach the legal age of adulthood, parents are not obligated to comply with financial and custodial requirements set down by the state. Some of these parents did not wish to be told how to care for their children. They are not stuck-like-Velcro couples, because they are not struggling. They have come to terms with their separation and their arrangements for children and are making a separated family life outside the legal system.

We were married and living together until 1985, but we were married 15 more years, legally married but no longer a couple. When we separated, we were both absolutely clear that we were not ever going to put the kids in the middle of a fight between us. In 1985 we had gone to see a mediator and wrote up a divorce agreement about property and money and to set down the custody arrangements that we'd agreed to. We'd made the plan work. And we never got around to filing it. If there are minor children in a divorce, you have to go through a court mediation process to make sure the children are safe. And I just never wanted to call up the court and make the appointment. I didn't want somebody I didn't know sitting and deciding whether or not we were doing a good job. We were just doing it. We finally divorced in 2000. (married 1970, separated 1985, divorced 2000, interviewed 2007)

Some parents feel no pressure to divorce because they have no wish to enter into a new legal commitment. They, too, live outside the legal system's accounting and the conventional statistics.

We're still not officially divorced. It will probably be pending forever. We still share the dog. He takes the dog on weekends when he can. We're financially all tied up, because we've shared his income since we separated. What I wanted from life was a family and community that I didn't have growing up. The longing for that never really left. So gradually, I began to bring him back for the family gatherings. His new partner is part of holidays, too. We just couldn't figure out how to divorce. (married 1973, separated 1995, not planning to divorce, interviewed 2008)

USING THESE PATTERNS GIVES A MORE NUANCED UNDERSTANDING OF FORMAL SEPARATION

These patterns of untangling, oozing apart, sudden splits, stuck-like-Velcro, and separated/still married are vivid descriptions of how parents actually move apart. My interviewees were looking back at least 10 years, sometimes 40 years. But, these patterns still ring true for couples I meet today. Knowing the patterns and hearing real stories are helpful to parents currently considering separation.

Recently, I sat in the warm sunset with a mother in Arizona. We watched her sons and my grandsons on the playground. She spoke of her troubled marriage and of the fears and choices about how to move forward. She wanted to know what my experience had been long ago, separating with young children. She was afraid of *separation*. She didn't want to "make a mistake." She saw her set of choices as black and white, yes or no.

Using the term "oozing apart" made sense to her. She had been thinking of separating for quite some time and had recently begun to speak about a formal separation in cautious ways. Many small separations had already happened. The parents had separate bedrooms. Friends knew of the struggles and of their in-house separation. As we talked, she warmed to the notion that separation was already a part of their relationship, neither a black-and-white decision nor a single moment in time. The sense of gradualness seemed to help her back away from a yes-or-no framework. She could see her choices with more complexity and ambiguity, always a sturdier platform to think through life choices and transitions.

Each of the small separations had its own consequences, and that process would continue. She could move slowly and carefully, giving up the notion that *separation* required a big and sudden move. She could focus on what she wanted and what she was willing to accept as the consequence of her choices. That both surprised and comforted her. Taking a more nuanced look at transition always means tackling ambiguity and complexity. Considering ambiguity and complexity makes a decision more realistic, and harder, than an all-or-nothing choice.[6]

Having a way to name a process of separation, of untangling, helped clarify the choices for this young mother in Arizona.

REARRANGING

Now on to the second task of separated parents: rearranging. After untangling, these parents went on to rearrange their adult lives and made a space for children in many creative ways. In the next chapter we pick up my story, rearranging after the formal separation in 1975. As you will see, the goal of the rearranging process is to create a benign emotional space for continued energy around the children. That is the space to continue to parent apart.

4

A Family Rearranges through the '80s and '90s

We had agonized around a kitchen table. We scratched the coating of the table and tried to understand. And then we moved away from that table, the table of so many questions. I uttered the words "I want to separate," and we moved into the dark unknown. My children's father found a room for a few days and then a nearby apartment. I saw that apartment once and was appalled—appalled that our civilization was so changed in that one moment. One sentence had ripped him out of a comfortable home into this small and sparsely furnished place.

Any life decision can bring mixed feelings. In our case, the oozing apart had turned from sadness to a moment of anger that brought many moments of regret and uncertainty.

We attended a family wedding about three weeks after he moved out. Together and surrounded by family, it was easy to want to spin the world backward. Driving home, I asked if he wanted to stay the night together. The "no" was another moment of separation. More anger, sadness, disappointment, and regret. In that moment, I knew that this was going to be our future—alone as parents. There was no denying that this was really happening.

Then we moved furniture. Moving the king-size bed was a powerful moment. Those king-size beds were new in the '70s. If you had one, it meant that you were a grown-up—and sexual. The shame of watching it go—and feeling like a failure—was more meaningful, more devastating, than the day in divorce court would be.

We were making it up as we went along, doing the familiar and day-to-day things of life with young children. We spoke daily, in person or on the phone (no e-mail then). He finished work about 3 P.M. and came to the house on some days. I'd go for a bike ride or to a class. Sometimes I'd stay away for a longer time. He'd feed the kids and give the baths and tuck them in. Then go back to his own apartment. Weekends were negotiated.

The first Christmas after separation, we spent together as a family. Out of habit, or the need to be with each other, we did what many newly separated families do. We gathered together again. What we had put in place was lonely, especially at family holiday times, and we needed some tradition to follow. We were together, and then he was gone again.

Each time I watched him go, I felt sad but safer. Some nights, I'd sit on the second-floor porch of the two-family house, enclosed by the trees, drinking a beer, trying to see into the future. It was quiet and lonely and sad, but it was also relieving to be away from all the conflict.

NEIGHBORHOODS AND GEOGRAPHY

We were one of the younger couples in our neighborhood in 1975. I knew that other marriages were rocky. One other couple had separated, briefly. Everyone else seemed to be staying together, doing "the right thing." A neighbor stopped by as I was gardening. He was very sweet and expressed his worries about both of us and the children. I was touched—and utterly help-less to know what other choices to make. I thanked him and tucked away his kindness.

None of us was aware of the tremendous wave of divorces that crested in the '70s and '80s.[1] I felt alone and unsure, with no models for how to go for-ward. We were the pioneers. And pioneers create ripples.

We had a group of friends—three families who spent lots of time together. Dinners, play groups, vacations. This group of six adults and six children were in and out of each others' houses and lives all day and all year. These couples were shocked and angry, mostly at me. But we stayed connected somehow. The grandparents and aunts and uncles were far away, so that network of families is what held each of us and let us be separated in our new way.

But our separation raised the question of separation in their lives and for others in the neighborhood. Everyone has to explain a separation—to him-self and to each other. And there was fear that "divorce might be catching." And in some ways it was. There was a lot of social permission to separate and divorce in those decades. The social messages from the 1950s were no longer primary.[2]

Since we both stayed in the neighborhood where our children were born and went to school, our lives were up for public inspection. The neighbor-hood first saw us as the young couple, then with a new baby, and then with two children. Now we were seen as "the separated couple." As the "roof came off our house," friends and neighbors had their own notions of what was hap-pening in our family life. Public scrutiny of family life is one consequence of separation.

The moment of public separation happened just before the opening of school in 1975, the very week our daughter started kindergarten. For me, tell-ing the school about the separation was filled with shame. My daughter was five. I was a stay-at-home mom, and she'd been in neighborhood playgroups and nursery school. But our family had never been seen in the ways one is "seen" when entering a mandated social institution. I felt I was to be evaluated as a parent. I trudged up to the kindergarten meeting and sat down with the teacher and said the words. Such waves of relief when she told me that she had divorced when her children were little. Okay, she'll look out for my daughter and maybe not judge me.

REARRANGING

Feelings and behaviors began to shift in ironic and curious ways. I had always been so vigilant and critical about how my husband related to the children, complaining that he wasn't very present when he was with them. Now that I was out of the way, he began to feel some confidence—enjoying his connections with them. Lots of fathers learn a lot about parenting when they experience a separation and divorce.[3] He began to find his way and felt more and more confident. When he could be a fully available parent to our kids, I had to learn to trust and rely on him in completely new ways.

I had been socialized to be responsible for how the family looked and worked. Women have had that task for centuries. But now I saw, on a daily basis, that he was able to care for the children both physically and emotionally and to provide safety and toys and food and toothbrushes at their other house. No reminders from me. I was relieved to not have the constant care, the role expectations. But at the same time, I felt excluded from that role and my familiar place. Ambivalence was weaving in and out again.

I struggled when I was too much in the middle, and I struggled with feeling left out.

NEW IDENTITIES

What would I do with myself? Experts say it takes about two years to move from thinking of yourself as a part of a couple to thinking of yourself as single again.[4] I had a lot more free time. I felt lonely and uncertain, and excited and uncertain. There were dark times of sadness and regret. There were new adventures in classes and connections. He often took the children up to our country house. That was sad and lonely for me. They were off enjoying our old life. He also had a new life in the city. What was he doing when he wasn't with the kids? I was jealous of his free time. I was jealous that he had work. And mixed about my stay-at-home decision. Mixed feelings weaving in and out again.

And yet, having young children often makes it easy to compartmentalize. There was so much to do that I found it easier and easier to set aside the old feelings of hurt and disappointment and guilt and sadness for stretches of time. Through day-to-day life, I was learning to trust him and trust myself in ways we had not been able to do while together. More benign feelings were growing.

It is definitely sad and ironic that we became better parents apart. We could support each other and live in different houses. No longer did we live with the tension of putting up a good front for other people and with the tension of the struggles about how to parent and how to use money.

It was easier to just be kind to one another. On one Mother's Day, I was surprised by him and two sleepy children, a large pot of flowers, and a big teddy bear. The teddy bear is one of my treasured possessions.

MOVING

I decided to move. Not far. Just down the street. I wanted to be out of the original family home. We still had that little house in the country and just fell into thinking of the place in the city as mine and the country house as his. I wanted a new beginning. There was an old Victorian house in the neighborhood. It needed a lot of work, so the price was reasonable. And there was a new government program (with 2 percent loans available) to bring existing housing up to code. I could fix up the house and think of it as my job for the next few years. Once it was renovated, I'd sell it for a profit.

We talked all this over. He agreed to help me with the financial and logistical details of a move. Although women had recently been allowed independent access to credit,[5] I didn't have a work history, so banks needed someone to cosign the mortgage. He had not a moment's hesitation about helping with this.

I moved. He helped carry boxes and toys. The kids were happy to be staying in the neighborhood. And happy to see us working together. A new start.

NEW RELATIONSHIPS

My former partner and I had each dated casually for the two years since our separation, but, in 1977, I met a man with two daughters. He was the minister in the local church and had recently had a difficult separation from his second marriage. I had started to sing in the church choir, and my first glimpse of him was looking down from the choir loft as he walked hand in hand with his six-year-old daughter. That was it. I loved that he took his daughter's hand. I wanted to find a new partner who was a committed father. I wanted to figure out how to have a big family.

I met the daughters of his first marriage one Sunday afternoon. They were 13 and 6, happily roller skating in the driveway. I remember looking at them and thinking this might be great. And, a moment later, thought this might be very hard. It was confusing and challenging to have conflicting needs and wants. That is the heart of stepfamily issues—trying to put together a new adult couple relationship and taking care of kids at the same time. Wanting the time to explore a commitment to another adult and having all the time demands of children makes for a very steep learning curve.

Daily living was complicated. I had no idea of the tensions and demands at that time. I still had a picture of a family that I wanted. But stepfamilies don't fit into the usual frames. "We all have a picture of family. It is not usually a stepfamily."[6]

My kids were four and seven, so there was a lot of balancing going on. I told myself that he knew about that balancing act of kids, former and new partners, so we'd work it out together. His children lived mostly with their mother, 20 miles away. They came on weekends and some holidays. He drove out to see them one weekday night. My kids and his kids were seldom at the same place at the same time. Scheduling and finding ways to cooperate had become central for me and my former and my new partners. To feel differing loyalties and connection toward multiple adults was a central part of the dilemma of our daily lives.

Throughout this new dating relationship, my kids' father was very supportive, and I was supportive of him. I was curious about his new relationships. We could be just pals again. Sometimes, we actually played a bit of golf together and, of course, continued to see a lot of each other at school and sports events. The kids continued to go back and forth several times a week, and we would see each other and chat during those times. We lived in the same neighborhood and he worked nearby, so there were also moments of unanticipated meetings in bookstores, at the post office, and at the local pizza place.

Still deeply committed to continuing to be the primary parents for our children and to having a continuing connection with each other, we were choosing new adult partners. It was becoming clear that another level of separation was emerging. Our paths headed further apart.

Into that mix came my former partner's new partner, a single woman. Her response to our close connection and cooperative parenting was confusion. New partners, especially new partners that are not parents, want a feeling of being first, of being chosen. And it's hard to feel chosen when there's all this busyness with small children and a former partner. The new partner without children is not first in anything—not first in getting time, or energy, or love. There is no easy path for women and men coming into a new relationship with a separated parent. When things work well between former partners, the single partner shakes his or her head and wonders, "If you're so close and do this so easily, why did you get separated?" Learning to live with all these old ties is perplexing for everyone in the family—the parents, the kids, the new partners, and the extended family. It can be perplexing for many years as this new circle of kin grows. It was no picnic for her.

So, our children now had two new and different couples in their lives. Even though the adults were "just dating," the stepfamily relationships had begun, and we all were learning to live with these new adults in our lives. The adults were sorting out things on two different levels: how to have time for the new intimate/sexual relationships, while doing the very busy tasks of looking after the children.

There was wonderful time alone when the kids went with their father. And there was also sadness and fear when I watched my kids go away. They were getting to know and feel loved by a very big family brought to them by their stepmother. New step-grandparents, step aunts and uncles, and lots of cousins. I had more time alone and yet learned the lessons of loneliness when the kids were away for the first time on Thanksgiving or a birthday, with others who loved and cared for them. Feeling left and lonely is a big part of life. Separations and stepfamily living can bring out those feelings in unexpected and challenging ways. It is important to learn that sadness, for parents and kids to learn to say goodbye and say hello in small ways, with safety.

LEGAL SEPARATION AND DIVORCE

By 1978, we both felt more confident in our long-term commitments to new partners and to having our kids have two parts to their family. We each began to talk of remarriage. Only then was it possible to turn to the actual question of our legal separation and divorce. The popular notion about separation and divorce is that it is a moment in time. In fact, my story and all the stories in this book demonstrate that the *moment* recognized by legal and social institutions is not as important as the *process of untangling and rearranging* that goes on for years, before and long after any legal and public moment. It was not until three years after publicly separating that the legal system intruded into our lives, that our personal lives and decisions became defined by the culture's words "divorced parents." The court and society would now see us only that way. When forms ask about family, there is no check box for "continuing to parent."

Because we'd been living this stable separated life and had built trust and predictability, we wanted to be careful about how the legal system would treat us. We were not arguing, and we did not wish to have lawyers arguing. We crafted a separation agreement with one lawyer and then used a second lawyer to look over the agreement as suggested. In 1978, no-fault divorce was newly enacted.[7] Mediation of parental agreements, so common now, was in its infancy. Joint-custody legislation had not yet been enacted in any state.[8]

We went to court together and sat next to each other for that powerful experience. It was solemn and serious and sad. We had that final legal and public ritual to share. But our court date was not devastating or furious or life changing. It was simply a legal matter. And a very important ritual for us. We had stood together in 1963, and we would stand together in 1978.

We became part of the statistics on that day, now three years after we had separated. As we walked down the courthouse steps, we had regained our sense of being supportive pals. And were living with the space of benign energy still connecting us. We lived apart. Our lives were running parallel, and we had similar requests of life: to work out life with new partners and to continue parenting and expanding the kinship circle for our kids.

After the one-year waiting period, we helped the children participate in two weddings. He helped care for our children on the days following my second wedding. Then, one month later, I drove with a friend to a town near the place of his wedding. My friend took my kids to the wedding of their father and stepmother. I took her kids to the park and a movie and had pizza.

In addition to their new stepmother, our kids also now had a new stepfather and two new stepsisters—and all the kin that comes along with each of those new family members. A whole new set of possibilities for Thanksgivings and birthdays. There are either twice as many people as you expected, or half as many as you may wish were there.

CHILDREN GROWING—MORE SEPARATIONS

The children grew out of elementary school and toward the teen years. Those years were filled with lots of readjustment and wondering which partner to talk things over with. Their father and I talked over the parenting stuff—ear piercing, curfews, how much of the city they could explore on their own, and what to do about forays into drinking. I talked with my new partner about how to sort out life in our home—dirty towels on the bathroom floor, putting dishes in the sink, noise, and friends visiting. Now there were many adults at parent-teacher conferences, at baseball games, at school plays. We all struggled with how to help them with sexual questions and dating. What would I tell them about relationships? I silently agonized and wondered about what they were learning from me and my life choices.

The children lived full time in my house. They went back and forth to their father's house regularly and frequently. We lived only a mile apart. In an urban area, a mile is enough distance—and enough closeness—to serve the many needs of this kind of separated family. And it gives the children some chance to work out their own comings and goings between houses.

When the children began to walk back and forth between my house and their father's house, there were no more casual connections at drop-offs and pickups. The child support checks began to be mailed, not passed in person. Very few logistical phone calls were necessary. These were moments of more separation for me, another loss. We needed to plan for holidays and vacations and sports and school events, but not in person. Our lives as parents to our children became more private and formal. After so many years of seeing each other multiple times in a week, we now had at least what society often sees as the traditional separation—very little adult contact.

UNTANGLING AGAIN

My second marriage began to unravel and crumble. Depression and alcohol abuse came into my life again, as it had been in my growing-up family. We did couples therapy, and I began to realize again that I could not make a family work without a full partner. My daughter was 16 and my son was 13 when we decided to separate, in 1986. I was thrown back into old questions: Who was I? And what was my life about? I had so wanted to make a family and here I was, again, a separated parent.

I had a new sad moment. I had to tell my children about this second separation by myself. Older kids ask more questions. You have to explain the whys and think much more about what is enough information or too much information. Their father was a big support to them during that time. It was his stable marriage that provided some foundation and hope, perhaps for all of us. It made me sad to know that I couldn't provide that kind of stability.

I had begun a counseling practice that was focused on understanding and supporting stepfamilies.[9] I had written a book about stepfamilies, and, ironically, my second husband had been the editor of that booklet. My practice was catching on as stepfamilies emerged on the cultural radar in the 1980s. I was becoming something of a "go-to person" about stepfamily issues and here I was, personally and professionally ashamed and sad and angry that I was unable to move through that process with my new partner. I could so easily describe this on paper and be so helpful in my office. Coming up against the complexity and ambiguity of one's own life is difficult, because we so often understand on an intellectual level what we are not ready to feel and cope with on an emotional level.

My second husband and I had no children together, so our separation, while painful, was quite unlike the first. However, now four children had their lives disrupted. All teens by then, they were trying to understand themselves and their own relationships. Now we asked them to untangle and rearrange again. In the teen years, most kids expect their families to stay boringly the same. And I wasn't giving that to my kids—nor to my stepkids.

REARRANGING AGAIN

My kids and I moved to a small apartment in the neighborhood. Again in a single bed, noticing the scrutiny of neighbors. And facing questions of work and financial stability for myself for the first time ever. There continued to be child support and a rather small income from my new therapy practice. But here I was, on my own again. And yet, not alone.

After separating from my second husband, I was able to turn to my children's father for some additional financial assistance. I can't recall if he wondered whether I needed money or if I just asked. But it was such a relief to be able to turn to him. I did borrow money to move and to establish a comfortable place for us to live. Looking to him for support was not a yearning to remake an old relationship but a turning to an old, trusted friend. He had been one of the pillars of my early life. What I wanted in life and what was true about life had been largely sorted out within the backdrop of that first relationship. Now I felt so grateful for our connection and the 11 years of solid co-parenting.

My former sister-in-law reached out to us on the first Thanksgiving after we moved out of the stepfamily home. We were welcomed back into what became a new family tradition for my kids and me. Their father and his wife had traditional plans with her family. The kindness of the embrace from my former in-laws helped heal the sadness and restore a sense of family. I was truly giving up the notions of what family is "supposed" to be. The family of kin did not divorce me, nor did my birth family ever divorce him. We were allowed to have our separation without sides being taken. Our kin understood how to stay connected to both of us.

GRIEF REVISITED

As the sadness of the ending of my second marriage began to find its place, memories of the abortion kept coming up in unsettling ways. Dreams and strong emotional upheavals at the anniversary of the abortion told me there was much that was not yet healed. Attending a professional conference, I heard of an ancient ritual, apparently from the Jewish tradition: take bread, cast it into running water, and pray for healing.[10] I asked if he would stand with me as I did this ritual. We had a very important lunch on the deck of a local restaurant that was right next to a lovely little waterfall. As I cast the bread, I felt more settled about that long-ago decision. And grateful that he was willing to stand with me once again.

AFTER THE LEGAL INK DRIES

Our legal ties were done when our children left for college. Child support stopped as each child turned 18. That was another poignant moment. First one and then the other regular monthly connection through the child support checks were gone. I hadn't expected to be sad about that. I wasn't sad about the money but sad about the lost connection.

But we had other connections. My former partner and his wife and I slogged through financial aid applications. My son went to college in 1991. The divorce rate was still very high.[11] But not for the parents at the little college he had chosen. As we gathered for a parent weekend, it seemed like kindergarten all over again. I felt the old shame from 1975 when I had to tell the kindergarten teacher of the separation. We sat at a lovely restaurant with my son's friends and their parents. Not one of them separated. And there we three sat together. Lots of discomfort for me. I asked my son at breakfast the next day what it had felt like for him. He looked at me in amazement: "It doesn't feel strange to me, Mom. I've had a lot of parents since I was two."

The next generation had adapted and could live with these new realities of family life.

And after my kids were done with college, their father and his wife moved away from our community. We'd all been just a mile apart for so many years, and now they were three hours away, in another state. That was truly a powerful change for me. Another separation in our parenting together. No more casual encounters. Children now had to make distinctly different trips to visit each of us.

WHAT MAKES IT WORK—OR NOT

All the threads of untangling and rearranging will feel familiar to separated parents. But each family weaves its own patterns. As the untangling takes many forms, so does the rearranging. It is wonderfully varied, as you will see from other stories in chapters 7 and 8. The rearranging does not have a single event as marker. A parent may choose to begin a new adult relationship or not. In either event, the separated parents continue to work out their relationship. New partnerships can help parents come closer, or, in some cases, a new partnership may mean more separation between parents—for a while or forever.

As children grow, parents continue to weave in and out of each other's lives. Having younger children at the time of separation often anchors parents in tasks and routines and schedules. A space for benign energy grows that can fill in around the spaces of hurt and anger. Having older kids at the time of the separation may make for a more private relationship with each child and a more formal relationship between the parents, one requiring little connectedness until the next generation comes along.

My untangling and rearranging did not involve a great deal of contention. Our grief, not our anger, was the center point of the separation. But, for many parents, there are years of battles in and out of courts. Some of the next stories paint pictures of more contentious untangling and rearranging. Most of the stories told here are of parents who were eventually able to come to some peace with their former spouses. Some simply made their own peace. Some came back into a comfortable place together as they understood what it meant to have grandchildren and to see themselves as kin.

Five factors pop up in the stories. They will be discussed more fully in the next chapter. The factors are all evident in my story. Geography is one. Staying in the same town allowed us to continue to care for our young children and to be a support and witness to each other's new partnerships and unfolding lives. We could rebuild our earlier trust as pals as we stayed close geographically. The neighborhood and familiar friends would be safe places for us to feel like our lives were continuous rather than abruptly changed. Once he moved to another state, we "heard" about each other rather than saw each other casually. A big change for me.

A second factor is the making of new relationships. In our case, both new partners were able to understand our continuing contact as a commitment to parenting, rather than as a threat to the new partnerships. Some parents do not have as easy a time as new love relationships come into being.

The most important factor in shaping relationships for adults and kids is the work the parents do to keep adult problems and conflicts from spilling onto their children. Over and over again the adults said, "It's not worth it, being so angry and sad all the time. It isn't helping me, and it certainly is not good for the kids." It is important to work toward letting go of the feelings of the anger and hurt and to move on to leave space for the more benign energy to grow. Children need parents who are speaking respectfully to each other, whether those parents are together or are parenting apart. Kids need parents who can take care of their adult problems and give kids the space to be children. They need parents who are healthy enough, emotionally and physically, to give enough attention to their children.

Long ago, I realized that I was never a single parent. I was a separated parent and I was single, but I was never parenting alone. When the media use the term "single parent," we need to be clear about what that means. Separated parents are not necessarily parenting alone.

Another language problem is the idea of "failed marriages" and how that term is understood in the larger society. My marriage ended but was not a failure. The goal of living together as a loving couple was set aside with sadness.

The next chapter, "Rearranging," considers how parents create benign emotional spaces for co-parenting and the five factors that help parents recognize kinship.

5

Rearranging

Rearranging is a challenge for separated parents. This is true as well for all parents.

Rearranging is normal. In a life with children, nothing is ever really settled. Once we get the hang of soothing a baby, the baby is off crawling and then walking—and then wanting to drive a car. All parents scramble along, learning what works at each new phase. Sometimes we have had good models for how to do this, sometimes not. All parents can evolve with their children. One has to work very hard not to change as a parent.

Separated parents have the added challenge of rearranging in two places around their children and continuing the normal scramble to keep up with them. As they make their formal decisions to separate, parents may not recognize how complex parenting can be from two households.

Initially, there is a sigh of relief. Something is done, and each may be eager to build a new life apart. At that point, the focus is on basic rearranging, moving the furniture and having physical space to parent the children without constant conflict.

Next are the more complex issues of how to co-parent from separate spaces and how to sort out the resources needed to continue to provide for children. Some separated parents begin new relationships quickly and have the added challenge of adding new adult partnerships to the kinship circle. The new partner has his or her own family ties, his or her own history, and his or her own needs for comfort and safety to add to the mix. All this goes into the rearranging.

As my story continued, there were many moments of rearranging, from moving a bed to a new apartment to sorting out the weekly schedule of childcare. And more complex moments of rearranging in second marriages and stepfamily living.

As I've lived my own story and listened to other stories, I find that the process of rearranging seems to have two parts. One part of rearranging is creating a benign space around the children. This *benign emotional space* is necessary to co-parent effectively. A second part of the rearranging process is *recognizing the lifelong kinship ties* between separated parents.

CREATING A BENIGN EMOTIONAL SPACE FOR PARENTING

A benign emotional space between the parents replaces the space of anger, sadness, and hurt of the lost love relationship. Creating a benign space is the goal for separated parents.

There are no requirements for the adult relationship other than to find ways to be effective as parents. Parents are most effective when they can create a space for their kids to grow and explore their own interests and talents. Children need emotional spaces separate from the problems of their parents. Kids can't solve grown-up problems. Grown-ups are supposed to solve grown-up problems. Kids need both of their parents, but not the problems. Grown-ups need to be healthy emotionally to be able to be creative about co-parenting. If the parents are emotionally healthy, they will be able to find ways to soothe their grown-up hurts and have energy available to care for children.

Creating benign emotional spaces is getting attention in the courts. Some judges build in space for parents to understand how important it is to work together before they will even hear the petition to separate and divorce.[1,2] This has proved effective in reducing the number of divorce cases that are litigated.

This benign space comes into being and flourishes for parents in moments of unconflicted contact: engaging in civil drop-offs and pickups, going together to parent-teacher conferences, cheering and groaning together at Little League games, watching a child's vigorous performance at a dance recital, cooperating in the college search. In all these places, the benign energy can grow. The adults get clearer and clearer that their old hurt feelings as lovers can be transformed into a new connection as parents. Benign emotional energy can fill the space between them as they build new trust in being parents together, replacing the lost trust as lovers.

This is also the space where one lets go of the way one wanted the other parent to be, allowing space for both parents to be themselves in the lives of their children.

Friends and family welcome this benign emotional space between the parents. They and the children are no longer apt to get caught in angry or tearful reactions or in the devastating experience of being asked to take sides in continuing tensions.

Think of the benign space as you would think of a diagnosis of a benign tumor. One doesn't want the tumor (the separation) in the first place, but it is such a relief to hear that it is benign. The goal in creating that space is not a return to a cozy relationship between separated parents. The goal is making space for a respectful relationship.

RECOGNIZING KINSHIP: STICKY, SILLY, AND SERIOUS TIES

In the flurry of activity around children, former partners keep bumping into each other. If they have small children, they may see each other multiple times a week. Or, if one parent is not able to be present for co-parenting, one bumps up against the absence. One way or another, it slowly dawns on most parents that the former partner will continue to be a part of their lives forever. Kids will continue to be in contact with the other parent—or may yearn for that other parent—forever.

Those sticky, silly, and serious ties form kinship. Some parents recognize their lifelong ties right from the start. Others come gradually to that awareness.

School graduations often provide the first visual invitation to experience kinship. Sitting in a long row of seemingly unrelated people, celebrating the accomplishments of a child, shows the kinship ties in public.

Some parents begin new families and recognize kinship only as new children are born into an extended family. Their first set of children welcomes new babies. Separated parents come to recognize and celebrate the kinship of multiple children from their first and second partnerships.

Some parents are freer to recognize kinship only after the legal and financial requirements are over. Notions about kinship really sink in when kids' weddings are planned or when grandchildren arrive. The separated parents now have an album of photos, proudly displayed, of weddings and baby showers. These are photos they might not have imagined—a rearranged family around their children—all kin.

> He's not somebody that I think of as out there, apart from me. When you described us as kin, that hit the nail right on the head. That's the way I feel. I want him to be healthy. I want him to be happy. I want him to be safe. I am very close to his wife. This is 28 years. (married 1964, separated 1978, divorced 1979, interviewed 2008)

FACTORS SHAPING RECOGNITION OF KINSHIP

The process of rearranging includes creating the benign space and recognizing kinship. Five distinct factors emerged in my interviews. These five factors contribute to the shaping of the benign emotional space and to where and how the kinship is recognized, appreciated, and passed along to the next generation.

The five factors are:

1. The impact of family life events. Births, deaths, weddings, and accidents are events that *require* families to rearrange.

2. The choices about where to live. Living nearby or across a continent makes different connections possible for adults and children. This is the *easiest* factor to understand.
3. Letting go of old hurts and angers. This may be the *hardest* task for the separated parents. But it is the most important for children. This is the core of the benign emotional space for parenting. Letting go allows children to have their own space to grow and develop and to have their own relationship with each parent. Children do not have to live within the shadow of a continuing war or with parents icily apart.
4. The demands and needs of new partners are *never neutral* in the re-arranging process. New adult partnerships always impact the benign space of co-parenting. Often, the impact is helpful. Sometimes, not so.
5. The age of children at the time of the formal separation is the *trickiest* issue to make any clear statement about. One thing is clear: separations when children are young allow more opportunities for the benign space to develop.

Factor One: Life Events Bring Recognition of Kinship

Life events shape all of us. Sudden accidents or death can have a dramatic impact on the connections in all families. Careful planning between separated parents doesn't prepare us for the impact of these sudden events. And there is no escape from their impact. Hearing tragic news about a child may bring separated parents to an instant recognition of kinship.

Something big did happen. I got a call about an accident. I don't remember whether I actually called my former husband, but within 10 minutes the four of us, he and I and our other two kids, were in touch with each other. Our son was paralyzed. I assumed that I would go to take care of him and that I would take care of everything myself. I had taken care of my father's dying myself, my mother's dying, my uncle's, and I just kind of assumed it was all going to be on me. Basically, I really felt like I was all alone in a family crisis. And then, when this happened, he came out to California right away. Then a few days later his wife and two other kids came to join us. I was amazed and pleased, very pleased. It changed everything for us.

We all stayed at my son's place. It was somewhat awkward, all of us sleeping on the floor. For that week and a half, we had a lot of contact. We had to figure out how to get the specialized treatments. And we had to find a surgeon. We started to get information about surgeons, and his new wife really got into that. She knows the medical system. We all got onto a conference call. His father and I, his stepmother, his brothers, his stepsisters, his doctors. We all helped him pick a surgeon. It was very respectful.

Other sad events gather separated parents. Historically, families have rearranged because of the deaths of parents in childbirth and in war. Children die in war, too. Being notified by officials of the death of a child in Iraq or Afghanistan has brought some separated parents to that moment of recognizing kinship. They were no longer separated adults; they were grieving parents.

The *Boston Globe* of April 3, 2006, reported on parents struggling to carry out funerals and memorials. The war in Iraq is the first war in which a large percentage of troops are from families of separation and divorce. Historically, the military assumed that the older birth parent (often the father) would be notified and had the right to make decisions about burial. Military protocol has been altered to honor the change in family demographics. Now, members of the military are required to designate a specific person who will make decisions about the remains and personal effects.[3] No longer is there an assumption of two-parent families.

The *Globe* article profiled one separated couple who for years had drifted apart in an alienated way. "Our divorce was horrible and everything, but when Nick was killed, none of that mattered anymore....It's about coming back together as parents. We supported each other through the funeral. We've supported each other ever since then."

Serious illness in a child or a former partner brings recognition of kinship, too. We never plan for our kids to be sick or in need of treatment. An important aspect of the rearranged family is a greater richness of resources. One family had need of resources when they learned that their adult daughter had cancer.

Now my daughter is undergoing treatment for breast cancer. We are all involved in the medical questions. Everything just changed, because her stepmother got involved. She's in the medical community, so she got my daughter in to be seen by the best people on a day's notice. That's a good part of the way this family works.

The personnel available for caregiving can be expanded. Aloneness is diminished as special ways of caring are welcomed by current and former partners.

Not long ago, my former partner had brain surgery. When he was in the hospital, I went in. His wife and I took care of him together. I'm a massage therapist, so I gave him a massage. I had to think more about boundaries, but it was very special to take care of him with her.

She has found ways to continue to participate with the new partner in ways that enrich all three of the adults and the children and grandchildren.

Other, more usual life events have the possibility of shaping how we see family and how we see our former partner. Kids' graduations are often one of those moments that open us to new connection.

At my daughter's graduation we hugged each other for the first time in years. I said, "We did it. They're all through school now!" That felt good.

How good it feels to be finished with the tuition payments! And how special to share that moment of relief. It is important for former partners/separated parents to find places to share their pride in having completed a part of their commitment to their children.

Religious rituals also frame our picture of family. In these rituals, families are asked to put the child in the center and work together in new ways.

An important event was Jacqui's Bat Mitzvah. I said, "Are we going to handle this like adults?" He had been divorced before, and when we were married we had to plan for the Bar Mitzvah of his first son. I watched as his ex-wife made it completely miserable for him. It was a horrible occasion. I didn't want a repeat of that. Even though we still argued quite a bit about our separation, we handled the Bat Mitzvah as real grown-ups. We had a joint luncheon. His family sat on one side. Mine were on another side, and the kids were actually in another room. It ended up that we got along very well. We're both proud of that.

Some parents cannot cooperate for these rituals, and the extended family and community of friends have no opportunity to celebrate the child.

We had a neighbor on the street who really wanted to do the Bar Mitzvahs with her ex, but he said, "Absolutely not!" We always did our Bar Mitzvahs together. Our kids seem to appreciate that we can do these celebrations together, because they see their friends who don't have family gatherings.

Rituals around the deaths in the extended family can also bring renewed connection for separated parents. Many spoke of the illnesses and deaths of former in-laws as significant moments of recognizing kinship. A former partner remembers our parents when they were young and healthy. Fewer and fewer people remember the vibrancy, or grumpiness, of our parents. It is meaningful and touching when someone can remember with us.

We're not uncomfortable in social situations any more. And we had been for a long while. Something changed when his mother was very ill. I'd known her for 40 years. I had a relationship with her. I knew that she was really very sick. I drove to North Carolina to see her and we had a very, very nice goodbye talk. When she died, I just decided for myself that I wanted to be at the funeral. I walked in and, when I looked around, I realized I had known her the longest of anyone in the room, aside from the direct family. It felt very right to be there. My former partner gave me a huge hug. Really genuine. And I think he felt very respected. Respected that I was there. Something changed then.

These parents recognized and began to respect each other as kin in the shadow of the death of a loved family member.

Religious holidays are also events of connection for the extended family. They can be the times that remind us to change our boundaries. To rearrange once again.

I did Christmas with his parents for years and years after the separation. We had the French Canadian tradition of celebrating on Christmas Eve. The next day, the girls and I would pack up and go over to his parents' home for Christmas morning. Sometimes he was there, sometimes not. He was a firefighter and had to work on some holidays. It wasn't until they were in their teens that I stopped that tradition. I changed my mind and began to take them over and stay only for a short visit. I would just give my greetings. I needed to change, but it was hard to do. It wasn't because of a new relationship for me or for him. It was actually for me to have some more independence, to redefine the boundaries again after we'd been separated for 10 or 12 years.

Sometimes, boundaries change to be more inclusive. Grown children have their own homes and begin to host the gatherings for family events and celebrations. Separated parents begin to be drawn into those new spaces, too. Having grown-up children brings new perspectives on the kinship circle, and their homes can be benign spaces for connection.

I see him more now when I go out to see my daughter and her family. There was a lot more contact with him after she moved into the family home when her grandmother died. He spends summers at that family home, so I see him and his girlfriend a lot in the summer.

And parents see each other in new ways as they independently offer support to an adult child. Realizing that a former spouse is right there beside them offering more support can soften the edges of a lot of hurt and anger and allow one to see the other as kin.

My daughter is a single mother by choice and moved back to our hometown to be closer to family when she had her baby. I had a welcoming party for her in her new home. I included my former husband and his wife. We hadn't socialized before that. I wanted them to join the party. Somehow, that cracked some ice. They invited me to their Christmas party that year. Since then, we both go if the kids have a party of one kind or another.

Being close to adult children in retirement is often on our minds as we age. As retirement comes closer and choices about where to live become urgent, the future may hold more surprising possibilities for rearranging the relationship with a former spouse.

We all might end up in the same city again. When I retire, I want to live near my daughter. He's thinking he wants to be close to her, too. I really don't want to be close to him, but it looks like he and his wife will be part of *my* retirement package. We do everything now as a family anyway. Christmas, Easter, Thanksgiving. So I can see us living close in two or three years. Is that odd? The next phase of life living close to him again. You really become family. That's important for me. I don't have much of a family, so I'm really feeling the need for family and connection. And that's one of the ways to do it.

Being reminded of kinship ties can come with seemingly small life events. When current news reminds us of old shared experiences, there is sweetness in being able to reminisce and hold the past without fear of disrupting current partnerships. Being free to reminisce means we can hold our own histories in a fuller way.

My new husband and his former wife had long years of connection around The Grateful Dead. When Jerry Garcia died, they just had to talk. They were on the phone for hours. It was lovely that they could share that. They have a strong commitment to each other. I really respect how they divorced and did parenting. It was nice to hear them having fun and reminiscing. They know each other so well.

Any life event presents us with the opportunity to change. Human beings have to work at staying stuck. Changing is what's normal.

Factor Two: Choices about Where to Live

Choices about where to live may be the easiest factor to understand. If separated parents stay close and have contact, it's almost certain that a new kind of relationship will be built, that they will see each other differently simply because they see each other often. Almost half of the separated parents interviewed for this book stayed in the same communities after formal separation. Most stayed until the children grew to adulthood.

At first, if separated parents stay in the same town, it may feel like an extraordinary burden. It may feel that they can never get away from the old life, from the old feelings. And some may feel judged about their decision to separate.

I grew up in this town for 32 years and did everything conventionally until I finally left the marriage. It certainly didn't sit well. There were a lot of whispers at the swim club. Today, nobody would blink an eye at our kind of arrangement [to co-parent and be friendly], but in the '70s, I was judged so harshly and shunned. (married 1964, separated 1978, divorced 1979, interviewed 2008)

Having more contact, the former partners and the extended family can begin to see connections change as the family rearranges and moves along through the years. Parents begin by having short, specific connections. Each moment of unconflicted interaction can bring a new aspect to a previously fraught relationship. Gradually, interactions become emotionally safe. The space for more benign energy grows to have new and different kinds of connections with a former partner. Parents leave behind the energy of their love relationship and move into a place of a more supportive parental connection.

Even at our worst, we co-parented well. She lived only a few blocks away. She had always asked for help around the house after we separated. Clearing out the gutters or shoveling snow. We really weren't getting along that well then. But I did it for her. Just the little things. I don't think the kids know that, how I helped their mother. I think it helped us all. (married 1978, separated 1988, divorced 1996, interviewed 2008)

Growing that new space for connection as parents is useful for everyone—adults, kids, the extended family, and friends. It may be hard to get there, but a new kind of trust can be established in that space. The edges of old hurts and fears can soften. Gradually, more and more safe territory, a bigger and bigger benign emotional space, can be created as parents stay close geographically.

Geography is pretty important here. If you're in the same place at the same time, something happens. That made all the difference. If one of us had moved away, this continued closeness never would have happened. We had mutual friends, so that was something that helped. We were both in the same community of friends. Occasionally, we would be at a party or at a football game. That was the real start in breaking the ice. It wasn't as if the four of us just suddenly said, "Let's have dinner." We stayed within 30 miles of each other all this time. Truthfully, we're friends now.

This set of parents hadn't intended the closeness. A natural flow guided them and their new partners to connect around the original two children and the two children born into the rearranged family.

I married about six months after the divorce, and he married six months after that. He married someone a bit younger, and they had two children. Our kids continued to go back and forth. My kids helped raise those two younger siblings. It's so peaceful and nice now that it's hard to remember back then. It was work, and it took time. (married 1964, separated 1978, divorced 1979, interviewed 2008)

For some parents, a close geographical connection is more intentional. One parent may have understood more fully the importance for kids of having easy access to both parents.

When we finally decided to separate, he said he was too busy to look for an apartment. One of the bravest things that I ever did was to force the issue of where he lived. I said, "Well, if you want to live at the house with the children, that's fine. I'll move out." I don't know how I had the courage to say that and take that risk. Immediately, he said, "No, no! It would make more sense for the children to stay here with you." So then I got to work. If he didn't have time to look for a place, well, I had time to look for him. I found this perfect place that he could rent with an option to buy. It was a quarter of a mile away. I wanted the children to be able to go back and forth. He liked it. It couldn't have been better.

The father did rent and later bought the house down the street. These parents have lived as neighbors for 25 years. Their compatibility is noticed.

One of my neighbors just thinks that he's the most charming guy she's ever met. She made some comment to him about our relationship, and he said, "Well, we have a better relationship than a lot of married people." Later, my neighbor said to me, "Boy, I don't see why you don't get back together with him if it's like that." I told her, "That's not the idea of what we want. It's working this way." (married 1975, separated 1985, divorced 1986, interviewed 2008)

Geographical closeness is not possible for some separated parents. Several parents started their families while living in Europe, married to European nationals. As the marriages untangled, they had strong pulls to return to the United States. They wanted to be closer to their own families and older friends. More support was possible for them in this country. They spoke about the challenges of rearranging across an ocean.

I was dedicated to trying not to make anything cumbersome for him and the kids. He would come here and he would stay here, at the house. I would either go somewhere or would stay home and work. A lot of people thought I was crazy to let him stay. But I thought that whatever could be done for him to see the kids was what was important. He was not a very present kind of father. Coming each year helps to keep him consistent for the kids. Ultimately, I wanted our kids to have their own relationship with him, so that's why I would let him come here. I would half hold my breath for two weeks while he was here. It worked. (married 1985, separated 1996, divorced 1998, interviewed 2008)

Geography can loosen ties, as well. At first, parents may rearrange to be near to each other. New life events make for difficult rearranging.

I was in the family home, and he had an apartment nearby. One son was living with him. But when he lost his job, he took off for California. I actually see this as the crucial final stage of the separation. It was a long time after the divorce. Basically he said, "I can't cope. Take him back. I'm out of here." He left, and then he quit paying the child support. I actually ended up going to the child support enforcement program, and for a while he had to have his wages garnished at his new job. Then I had to scramble my way to full-time work. (married 1965, separated 1987, divorced 1990, interviewed 2006)

The long-term impact of where we choose to live is not always fraught with conflict and hurtful emotions. It may simply result from changes as we retire or as our children grow into adulthood.

Now our relationship is more distant. We have no reason to talk anymore. But when we do talk, it's friendly. He just moved back home to the islands. Before that, he was almost around the corner. I haven't heard from him since he moved, but my new husband and I are planning to go to the islands this Christmas. I'll just give him a call or show up on his doorstep. I'm sure I'll run into family and people that I used to know. I wonder what that's going to be like. (married 1979, separated 1991, divorced 1994, interviewed 2008)

Choosing to live close can compromise privacy. Separated parents often know a lot about each other's new lives. That can be quite complicated or annoying or sad. At the very least, mixed.

His wife is coping with breast cancer now. I gave her a referral to a therapist in the building where I have my office. This is a small town, so sometimes I see them in the waiting room when I'm going to work. (married 1979, separated 1987, divorced 1987, interviewed 2008)

Like family connections, friendships from the first relationship can remain strong and are more overlapping if the separated parents are in the same town.

Our old friends were more identified as my friends, although everyone is very fond of him. Whenever we do social things, I frequently ask him to come over, and my friends are always thrilled to see him. His high school friends are happy to see me, too. I don't feel any discomfort when we meet up with each other. (married 1970, separated 1978, divorced 1981, interviewed 2001)

Sometimes, even a former wife and a current wife find ways to forge a friendship that would not have happened had they not been in the same community.

After my stepdaughter's Bat Mitzvah, her mother called and said, "Hey, do you want to go for a walk?" She had just ended a nine-year relationship and was brokenhearted. I think I walked her through the grief of that breakup. We walked and walked and walked all summer and all winter. My friends thought it was very odd for us to be so close—the former wife and the current wife. But we had learned to work together, and I felt so close to her. (married 1970, separated 1978, divorced 1981, interviewed 2001)

Living in a small town or in the same urban neighborhood brings an added dimension to these kinship ties. It's like having all your cousins down the street. Hard to get away from everyone's assumptions and opinions. It is a challenge to dodge opinions of others, the biases of society and of friends and family.

The task of being a parent is an evolving one. We grow into it. We grow into a wisdom that grows as we continue to care for children and stay open to each other. All parents keep their fingers crossed, wondering about choices and consequences. It's no different for separated parents living in the same town or across a continent.

Factor Three: Letting Go of Old Hurts and Angers

"We moved from cool to civil, and now we're coming into cordial." Many separated parents reflect this sentiment. Letting go of old hurts and angers, recognizing the regrets and sadness, may be the hardest task for separated parents. Letting go has the biggest payoff for the children. Popular culture expects hard feelings and doesn't help us much with endings or sadness.[4] In public opinion and in the media, it seems easier, and more acceptable, to be angry than to feel just plain sad.

When we understand feelings of sadness and loss, we understand ourselves and our situations more fully. *Knowing* our many and conflicting feelings is helpful. *Acting* out the feelings is what causes trouble. Being reactive to our feelings is what gets us into trouble. We all have lots of feelings. Some feelings we like; some we don't. Knowing all the mixed feelings, not staying stuck in anger or sadness, makes us stronger.

It's often confusing when one is told to just feel the feelings and let them go. I think of trees. Gentle breezes move through the branches of a tree. The winds from violent storms also pass through the branches, letting the storm move through. Sometimes, a tree is blown down. But, more often than not, the tree may twist and bend but find a place of rest again. Letting the mixed feelings flow through is the task. Trying to stop the wind does not work. Acknowledging our mixed feelings about a former lover helps us gain a foothold on how to commit to co-parenting. We allow less space for the old angry, sad, and hurt feelings and free up more benign space to co-parent and to perhaps feel the warmer connections to each other.

Slowly letting go of being *partners and lovers* and recommitting to being *partners and parents* is the single most important factor in the lives of the children. The space for benign energy grows and opens respectfully around the tasks of caring for children.

Long ago, in a children's workshop on divorce, I watched as kids talked over their experiences living through their parents' separations. They discussed, in very deep ways, what they wanted their parents to know. Touchingly, the children agreed on this: *"Tell me you love me. Don't use me in a tug of war."*

All children need parents who speak respectfully to each other. Sadly, this is often not the case. Whether parents are together or apart, children do best when they can count on their parents to be grown up, to set aside conflict about adult issues, and to take care of the adult problems like grown-ups. All families have problems. Separations are a grown-up problem. Children cannot solve grown-up problems.

Coming to terms and understanding our mixed feelings can show our kids how to be grown-ups who are not afraid to tackle grown-up problems.

Coordinating is relatively new for us. He lived far away for a while. When he moved back into this area, I screamed at him a lot. I was so angry about the way he had left. But as I screamed and I got more comfortable with my strong feelings, things changed. The kids saw that they could trust that we were going to be okay being together. Now there's a comfort. It feels as if everyone's comfortable. Fifteen years into it, and it got comfortable. (married 1965, separated 1987, divorced 1990, interviewed 2006)

Some parents can let go of old feelings early in the process of rearranging. They understand that carrying the hurt and anger and sadness isn't useful for them or for their kids.

> Part of what made it so peaceful between us was that I said, "I'm out of here and don't want anything." I don't know where we would be if I had fought about money. Maybe things would have gotten peaceful but maybe not as quickly. Also, there's not been much anger or regret because we both remarried within six months. If we had remained single maybe that would have been a different thing, but we each had somebody else. I certainly wasn't going to get involved in a lot of anger, because I didn't want to hurt my new partner. We each had partners, and that stopped us all from acting out the old feelings right then and there.

This woman was strategically smart in the first years of rearranging. She was fully aware that reciprocity and respect for each other's needs would be central to any negotiation in future. She told of an important moment, a shaping phone conversation early in her separation. She called to ask her former partner to make a change in the children's schedule. She got a resounding *no*. Instead of fighting, she floated the notion of future needs. He got it.

> It didn't move smoothly in the beginning. I planned a party for my new husband's birthday. That turned out to be on the day that the kids were supposed to be with their dad. When I asked to make a change in the schedule, my ex told me he was sticking to his day. Our separation was brand new, and I didn't want to fight. So I said, "Okay, well, there's the outside chance that one of these days the kids will be here with me, and it will be something important to you." That was the end of the conversation. We hung up. He called me back in about 20 minutes and said, "I get it. Okay." That was the turning point. There was understanding after that. We learned quickly how to be flexible. (married 1964, separated 1978, divorced 1979, interviewed 2008)

Parents disagree all the time, and separated parents are no different. But, they may not have learned how to fight fairly. Often, there is loudness in letting go of the old, hot, adult feelings. Space for intense anger and sadness helps us know how to understand and change.

> He knew I was angry. He started not answering the phone if I called him at night or early in the morning. Eventually, I said, "We're sharing two children. I'm only calling you if I need you for something regarding them. You'd better answer the damned phone." I did get over the worst of the feelings of betrayal over the relationship as we had to talk about

the kids so much. I found my voice after I separated from him. It took a while, but I found my voice. And it was a voice I never had before. I had to split from him in order to become my own person. I could never fight with him until we got divorced. When I stood up for myself and was really forceful, he really paid attention and respected me. It had an impact. (married 1968, separated 1980, divorced 1981, interviewed 2008)

And even when a solid co-parenting partnership has been established, the parents may still have specific conflicts. Creating the benign space does not mean an absence of conflict. Conflict is a part of life.

For some parents, the benign emotional space develops in a more professional setting. The adult son in this family began therapy long after his parents had separated. He had his own questions about life and adult decisions. By going into therapy himself and asking them to participate, he stumbled on a way to help his parents develop a more useful connection. His mother told of her experience of this family change.

There was lots of anger in the beginning when we separated. We were in touch when the boys were growing up, but I wanted to be very separate from him. One thing seemed to help us see each other differently. We had contact when our son started talking to a shrink. He wanted to tape conversations with each of us and to visit his grandparents' graves. He brought us to some sessions. We did all that together. I think we felt a benign energy toward each other through all of that contact and shared history. (married 1963, separated 1978, divorced 1980, interviewed 2007)

There are other ways to let go of negative feelings. One parent can let go, alone. Sometimes, therapy is a useful vehicle for letting go if the other parent is unable or unwilling to help create a stable benign space.

Now that I'm not bound to him, I'm able to say he's a curious, interesting guy. But, boy, he doesn't know how to do this relationship thing. That's easy to say now. I was in therapy on and off for a couple of years. That helped a lot. I called my therapist a "forest guide." She really helped me find my way through all sorts of things that enabled me to help the children. I learned how to help myself, and then I could help them. It was absolutely helpful to have a therapist validate the situation for me. The therapist's words sort of helped me realize it wasn't my fault. I still need to balance my need to know what's going on with the kids and not get poisoned by anger and stress and disapproval of the way he handles himself with them. He just wanders and is a free spirit. There's no renewed closeness between us as adults. I don't respect him. But I've learned how to not be stirred up by him or critical all the time. (married 1985, separated 1996, divorced 1998, interviewed 2008)

Grandchildren soften old feelings. We see them and remember other parts of our life together. We wonder anew about how we are all connected. Grandchildren invite us into new spaces around them.

But this last year, I feel I've just let go of all the negative feeling, the bad feelings. I don't call him up and have friendly chats, but we do communicate with each other around the children and that feels good. We can talk about the children and more comfortably now about the grandchildren. We have a little bit more sympathy, a little more friend- liness around our babies. (married 1967, separated 1994, divorced 1995, interviewed 2006)

Most parents said they let go of old and destructive feelings and behaviors because they wanted to feel better about themselves. Carrying old angers and hurts felt damaging to them in the present. They wanted a more benign space for themselves, not just for their children.

I never wanted to be a bitter and angry person. Those first years were very hard. I tried my best to keep the peace because that was what I felt was important. But there were times that I sacrificed my own needs. Sometimes he made me so goddamn angry. At some point, it felt point- less to stay angry. I don't know where it gets you. (married 1970, sepa- rated 1978, divorced 1981, interviewed 2007)

Many reflected this sentiment: "If we'd stayed married, it might have been a very angry but long-lasting marriage. But now we're mutually supportive of our sons, and friendly." Letting go and moving brings more gifts than it costs.

Factor Four: New Partners Are Never, Ever Neutral

Each new partner views the former relationships of separated parents and children through his or her own lens. Early on in any new partnership, there is a need for space for the people involved to become a couple.[5] But, leaving space for the new adult partnership to grow may infringe on and impact the benign space previously created by the separated parents.

The demands and needs of a new partner have a profound impact on the way the separated parents continue their relationship. Adding a new partner to the kinship circle can be very helpful to everyone. And it can make for new divisions and complications. It is never neutral.

Sometimes, finding a new partner can make the rearranging much easier. Gloria shared a "modern" moment in her rearranged family.

I am friends with his wife. She took a great attitude right from the beginning. We've had 28 years being together so far. Recently, we were planning a party for one of our kids, and I was at their house and the two of us were sitting in the kitchen and having some wine. He came in and said, "Oh, this is perfect. My two wives drinking wine and trashing me." And we both said, "You are so right." And that's where we are. As trite as it may sound, we're friends. It might be hard for anybody else to understand. (married 1964, separated 1978, divorced 1979, interviewed 2008)

And, sometimes, finding new partners can make family life much more difficult. Separated parents may have found ways to work together early in the rearranging process at a time when neither had a partner. Adding a new partner always means that the space between parents has to be renegotiated.

He took care of our little girls on the evenings I was working. I would stop and pick up my daughters after work. Things were okay until he started to date the woman he later married. Dating changed everything. Initially, I didn't know that he was dating. Then suddenly, when I stopped to get my daughters, instead of inviting me inside the house, he'd leave me standing on the front steps. He wouldn't make eye contact with me. Then I found out from the kids that he was dating. I think she didn't like our friendliness.

Now that he's remarried, it's been extremely difficult. She won't acknowledge me. We went through several graduations where we weren't sitting together. She wouldn't directly return my hello. She treated me as if I wasn't there. I know it sounds as if I'm bashing her, but this is really how things played out. In 2006, at college graduation, we were on the front porch of my daughter's dorm—all of us. When he and I were friendly to each other, she went storming off. Now, he basically won't talk to me. I've had conversations with his sister, and she said that his wife told him that there would be hell to pay if he had anything more to do with me. It's really, really sad. I mean it's uncomfortable for me, but it's particularly sad because it makes it so difficult for the kids. (married 1975, separated 1993, divorced 1997, interviewed 2009)

When new partnerships form, there are fears on both sides. New partners who have never had children may fear being sidelined, that they will have no standing in their new partnership. They may fear not having the authority or the temperament or the skills to be a parental figure.

He eventually remarried. On the one hand, it got somewhat better after that. And, on the other hand, this woman, for some reason, seems to feel threatened by me. She doesn't have any kids. There are some times when it would be really nice to do things together, and she puts the ki-bosh on that. She struggled with coming to an engagement party at my house. At my son's college graduation, we all went out to dinner with my parents, but there is no predicting how things will go. (married 1970, separated 1985, divorced 1988, interviewed 2008)

This woman has no way of knowing what is going on in the mind of her former partner's new wife. She just experiences the increased tension on oc-casions that were once easy. This new relationship is only a few years old, so tensions may ebb as the new partner feels more comfortable.[5] The issue can't be directly addressed by her former partner. He or she may not experience the tension or feel uncomfortable discussing it with his new partner. This is one of those fuzzy places that come as the rearranging continues. It is best to see it as a part of the process and know that it will likely change again. There's no guarantee, but the odds are in favor of change. Relationships may get easier. They may get harder. One can't predict the direction of change, but it's easy to predict change of some kind.

One parent, often a person who does not have a current adult partner, may fear that the new couple will create a family space that is much more appeal-ing to the children. They fear a loss of connection, of "losing" the child to the new family. Or they fear that any new children will upstage or complicate life for the first set of children, complicate a delicate balance already achieved.

My big threat is that he would have other children who would edge my kids out. I didn't have any relationships for a while, because the chil-dren were living here and I thought it was very important not to have other men in their lives. He did not feel the same way. He had various girlfriends along the way. He now has a sort of once-a-week girlfriend whom he also goes on trips with. He seems to be quite fond of her. I get insecure if I ever think he's going to get married. A new partner would rock the boat, because we're so very close. Two years ago, each of us had a significant surgery. We were the ones taking each other to the hospital and being next of kin for each other. I don't know whether a wife would be comfortable with that. I don't want my kids to have to deal with a new wife, either. (married 1975, separated 1985, divorced 1986, interviewed 2008)

Who takes the lead in trying to sort out how the parents operate with new partners and how the adult relationship boundaries get established? The sepa-rated parents? The new partners? Everyone may have strong opinions—and conflicting ones.[6]

My former husband always made it clear to whomever he was dating that he and I were very good friends and that they needed to accept, from the get-go, that we were going to have a relationship. That kept me going. I couldn't imagine that he would be out of my life. Then, I knew he didn't have to be out of my life. That made a big difference. He said to his dates clearly that we had a relationship, not romantically of course, but our family was a priority.

Then he married someone who had no children. They still have no children. When it comes to the kids, we know how to keep things straight. When he and I have to talk about the kids' welfare, his wife knows when to leave it to us. If we ask for her opinion, then she will give it. (married 1968, separated 1991, divorced 1994, interviewed 2009)

These parents have created clear boundaries and lines of authority. All families struggle with questions of authority and how to discipline. Stepfamilies usually have a tough time with these questions. What is usually helpful is to think of two kinds of authority. One kind of authority is around the children's personal choices and freedoms. The other authority is around the children's use of space in the home of either parent.

The separated parents have authority and manage discipline in the personal realm—medical issues, schooling, drinking/drugs, piercings. Stepparents give advice and often become trusted parental advisers. But it's important to know the line drawn in the preceding comment. "When he and I [the parents] have to talk about the kids' welfare, she [the stepmother] knows when to leave it to us. If we ask for her opinion, then she will give it." These are parents and a stepmother who understand the essential boundaries in these kinds of families.[6] The separated parents make decisions around the children's welfare, safety, health, and education.

The second area of authority is in the new couple connection. The parent and the stepparent have authority within their own home. The new couple has authority over the space they make for themselves and the children. It's important for new stepparents to be authorized to call the shots on how the new household runs and how the space is used. Wet towels on the floor, noise too early or too late, dishes in the sink, mealtimes, respectful language—all these are part of the daily routines of a household, and the adults who live there have the power and responsibility to decide and enforce standards. The parent must give his or her new partner, the stepparent, the authority to make and enforce those standards, as well.

Some new adult partnerships bring wonderful three- and four-parent stepfamilies into being. They are new extended families that really work. Some former and current partners become quite close. Their temperaments mesh easily.

My former husband met and moved in with someone rather quickly. I heard about her from the kids. I knew they really liked her. She was an important part of their lives. For me to stick my head in the sand wasn't going to work. I initiated the contact between us. I had to get to the point that I was ready to initiate it. She said later, "If you hadn't, I would have." But it was easier because I did it. I called her up and said, "There are two reasons that I'd like to get together with you—those two boys." We got together, and we talked and talked.

Now, I'm closer to his wife than to him. I care *about* him. I don't care *for* him. She says we are "sisters-by-divorce," because we really are good friends. It's been wonderful having an extra parent. Most of the negotiating is with her. We planned both kids' weddings, a brunch afterward for one son, and the rehearsal dinner and the brunch for the other son. It was lovely. (married 1966, separated 1995, divorced 1996, interviewed 2007)

Some separated parents are touched when new partners are added to the kinship circle, new adults to love their children. They enjoy watching loving relationships develop between stepparents, children, and grandchildren.

What's so beautiful is that we do have these grandchildren and we get together for holidays. My former husband's new wife has never had children, although she was married and divorced before. Now she has these babies, our grandchildren, and she can dote on them and shop for them and love and play with and sing to them. And I think that's beautiful. (married 1968, separated 1991, divorced 1994, interviewed 2009)

And, of course, some of the adult ties are quite limited because of the personality and temperament of a new partner. Every family has someone who is difficult and/or annoying. Families learn to be creative about dealing with them. One important fact is to remember that difficult or annoying relatives often care deeply about our children.

He's the friendliest guy. We have such a good time. His second wife is part of the fun, too. It works really well most of the time. Not so good when I'm in her house. She's quite anxious and quite controlling when anyone is in her house. When we're out together, it's easier. I like her. I don't feel jealous or any animosity toward her. I was relieved in a way because he's disorganized, and she had a way of organizing his life when the kids would visit. She had never married nor had kids. And she was devoted to our kids. I mean what could be better, right? I've learned to deal with her. (married 1970, separated 1984, divorced 1989, interviewed 2009)

Some former partners are not able to have a relationship after they separate. They have not recognized kinship ties to each other, publicly or openly within the family. For a separated parent in that kind of situation, a new partner may be able to bridge the old wounds and help to rearrange the ties between parent and children. With a new partner's help, they can soothe old hurts, let go, and get back to the job of being a parent.

My new wife has never met my first wife. They wouldn't even know each other if they were in the same room. It always worked out that they never met. When I left my first wife, my son wasn't talking to me because of loyalty to his mom. My new wife didn't like that and encouraged me to call. After I'd been remarried for three years, my son and I started talking on the phone. Then we'd go to see them as a couple. We helped them work on their house. I'm glad I made the first move to get back in touch with him and that has been the right thing to do. But my new wife was the one who has helped me mend the hurts with my kids. (married 1961, separated 1987, divorced 1988, interviewed 2006)

Another testimony to the healing possible with a solid new partnership comes from a father who was estranged from his kids and his kids' three different mothers for many years.

There is one point that is important. The fact that I remarried, now for 20 years. She has supported me with my kids, and I have supported her with her kids. I'm not known as Paul to her kids. I'm known as Dad. So they come to me a lot. If you're lucky enough to be remarried and you're lucky enough to have someone to work with you in the relationship, it does make a big difference. I never had that with my kids' moms, so I'm lucky that my wife helped me get back in touch. (married 1961, separated 1973, divorced 1974, interviewed 2010)

Factor Five: Ages of Children at the Time of Separation

This is the trickiest of the factors. Most parents wondered whether they did the right thing in separating at all. They wondered whether it would have been better to separate when kids were young. Or to have waited until they were of adult age. Remember, it is the age at the time of the formal separation that may have the greatest impact, not the age of the child at the time of divorce. The child's *age at separation* and *age at divorce* can be quite different, depending on adult decisions.

Historically, children have had to deal with family rearranging after desertion of a parent or death of a parent in war or childbirth. There were no choices about age in those sad circumstances. When there was rearranging due to desertion or death, there were varying degrees of success for these rearranged families. The same thing is probably true about the age of the children at the time of the formal separation and/or divorce.

On one hand, separating when children are little may mean kids get less attention as parents become preoccupied with untangling and rearranging their adult lives. And, on the other hand, separating when children are older may mean that the kids grow up with parents who live together but are constantly and angrily focused on each other, with little energy for family life. That may be just as draining for children as learning to live in two households with less tension.

EXPERT ADVICE

Experts have given contradictory advice. Parents have been advised to stay together for the sake of the children and, on the contrary, to separate when children are young, sparing them years of living in tension-filled homes.

Experts once advised parents to make a complete split if they had to divorce. A prominent journal suggested that it was not in the child's interest for both parents to continue their involvement with each other after a divorce.[7] The journal was published in 1977. Now, of course, we see that advice as completely unhelpful to parents and to kids.

Professionals, the media, and many institutions of the larger society have much to say about children and separation and divorce.[8] Much was helpful. Some of what was published in the '80s scared parents. The parents interviewed for this book have lived through the debates and the changes of the past 50 years. As they were wrestling with their own separations and divorces in the '60s, '70s, and '80s, states were enacting joint-custody legislation,[9] making it possible for these kinship connections to be recognized, for parents to have the legal option to continue to work together. Joint custody allowed parents, these pioneers, to feel successful, not "broken" or "failed." The demographics of the family changed. Family change and language outpaces the professionals who study family. We now see the change and live with the many ways that families look today.

Many parents I interviewed for the book said this: "I think separating when the kids were young made it easier." There was more time for finding a way to work as co-parents and more time for the benign energy to grow during the early school years. The school years presented parents with opportunities to be together at performances and sports events, in unconflicted situations. There is more time to learn how to move from the tensions of untangling to a more solid, rearranged connection as separated parents. When new stepfamilies are formed, there is more time to build safety and become comfortable together as new traditions are established.

Other parents separated when children reached their teens. One woman reported having a solid and connected and unconflicted experience with her partner during the years when the kids were little. Their family life as a couple and as parents was full and rich. That changed as the kids moved into more independent lives in the teen years.

Then the boys got to be teens and were off with their own friends and their own interests in the world. They didn't want to spend time with us doing family things any more. My husband and I looked at each other and realized we wanted very different things as individual adults. We had that wonderful family time when the kids were little. We really had something special as a couple with the boys. And then we didn't when it was just us.

Having teenagers confronts adults with many questions about life. As teens go off into their own interests and their own social world, we return to old questions about meaning and what we want from life. Sometimes, this is what makes having teens so unsettling. Teens challenge us just because of their age and their place. They are just beginning their journey into the grown-up world, just as we are realizing that we are at the midlife point. This particular couple did separate and found it relatively easy to create the benign emotional space to continue parenting, because they had had such a rich experience together for so many years.

After we separated, we had some early anger and certainly some sadness, but it was easy to remember how much we respected each other as parents and to find that closeness and kinship again. (married 1974, separated 1995, divorced 1998, interviewed 2006)

People who "stayed together for the kids" reported long, energy-draining years of indecision that drew as much attention from children as an actual separation. After separation with older kids, there are fewer occasions for the parents to have unconflicted contact. There is less opportunity to move into the benign emotional space. Parents may still be wrangling as children marry or as grandchildren come into the family circle. One separated parent who waited until her children went to college had this to say:

My kids were children of a very quiet, unlively household, not children of divorce. We don't know what that means to them yet. Perhaps we should have separated earlier. I could not do it. Now I have so many more models of friends who have done this. They found ways to make it work, made new models about kids and separation. The old model of simply staying 'til they were grown was ridiculous for everybody. All the hostility made it hard for any of us to live fully. (married 1969, separated 1996, divorced 2009, interviewed 2010)

And, of course, many parents wait until children go off to college or into adult work. I have had many clients who come into therapy to sort out their own adult relationships and quickly tell me about the legacy of their family's separation and divorce. One young woman had parents who "stayed together for the kids." She learned of her parents' separation just before Thanksgiving of her freshman year in college. It came as a complete surprise and started, for her, a long and sad revision of all of her family experiences. She did not know what to trust about her history, or what to trust about her parents or about their relationship with her or with each other. In therapy, this young woman agonized over whether she was to blame for her parents' unhappiness. "Why did they stay for me? I should have kept them together. I failed. It was just too much."

Whatever the age of the children, there are costs and benefits for adults and children. But the age of the children at the time of separation may not be the most basic question. We may need to look more at the child's temperament, resiliency, and other factors to predict how kids will manage their parents' separation.

TEMPERAMENT, RESILIENCY, AND OTHER FACTORS

Central to any discussion of the impact of separation and divorce is the reality of each child's temperament and how children react to transition. While age is one concern, the impact of parents' separation can never be reduced to a simple notion of chronological age as a guide to the best time to separate. Children in the same family react in a variety of ways. Age is not the only predictor or guide. The temperaments of some children seem to make them invulnerable to family change. They roll with all sorts of difficult situations. Other children have a more fragile temperament and are easily wounded by even the slightest change in the family.

Birth order may need to be considered. Older siblings may escape the family tensions as they grow and go off to college or work. Or the littlest child may have no memory of tensions experienced by parents. Either they were protected by older siblings, or the separation happened before they absorbed too much of the emotional climate of the family.

Whatever the ages of the children, there are other important factors in how kids adjust to parental separation. Each parent has a unique relationship with each child. As the adults untangle, mothers and fathers experience changes in the ways they relate to their kids and to the mother/father role. We all become a bit unfocused in our parenting skills at the time of separation, but it is important to find ways to regain that focus. Some parents learn to have more time and attention with their children. Mothers and fathers learn new aspects of their roles as they learn to have time for caregiving and work responsibilities in separate homes. The important thing for kids is that one or both parents continue to be available and predictable and emotionally healthy. Children need at least one parent to come to terms with the problems and losses and return to normal functioning as quickly as possible.

LESSONS LEARNED

When clients come into my office, I always ask them what they learned from their parents and how they are repeating their parents' patterns in their own lives. I am always thinking about the generation before and the generation to come, trying to help them find words so that conversation can begin.

I ask the same question of young single adults who are not in a relationship and of couples who are in deep conflict. Often, it is a surprise to them to begin to see that they are repeating family patterns unconsciously. They may not have learned how to fight fairly in their family. They may not have grown up in a family in which parents continued to be sexually committed after kids were born. They may not have learned how to rethink roles for parenting. Or how to change expectations about what children need.

For couples who come into therapy as they consider separation, I first get a sense of their conflicts and how they speak to each other and how they listen to each other. Then I ask pointed questions: "What do you want your children to learn about being married? About being a parent? About being a grown-up? About how to fight?"

Most people are surprised when they stop and think about this. They recognize immediately that they are presenting a picture that is not very helpful. They had not even considered what the children were learning. They simply tend to think their children were not noticing or not hearing or not seeing what is going on with them as a couple.

But, our children are always watching us.

So, if parents are going to separate, the question may not be what age is best for children. It may be, What do you want your children to learn about how to live a full life? What do you want your children to learn about how to look for and find a loving, safe, and comfortable adult relationship? What do you want your children to learn about being a parent and resolving conflicts? How can you best prepare your children for a life full of their own rearranging?

Rearranging in families goes on and on. The most important aspect for separated parents is how to approach the goal of creating a benign emotional space around their children. It doesn't simply happen because time passes. Parents work at creating this space together or alone. Having the space and recognizing kinship through children will enhance life for everyone—adults, kids, the extended family, and friends. The truth is that separated parents will be tied together in sticky, silly, and serious ways forever. Once that is recognized, everyone can continue to grow.

The five factors have differing importance and significance in the shaping of the kinship circle. Briefly restated, they are:

1. Life events always bring family together in some way. Births, deaths, weddings, and accidents *require* families to rearrange.
2. The choice about where to live is the *easiest* factor to understand.

3. Letting go of the old feelings from the loss of the love relationship may be the *hardest* to do. However, letting go is the only way to create the benign emotional space to effectively co-parent. It is the children's birthright.

4. The choice for new partnerships is an unpredictable factor. The demands and needs of a new partner may be helpful. Or, they may be very disruptive. They are *never neutral*. Each new partner views the relationship of separated parents and children through a unique lens. Early on in new partnerships, there is a need for space to form around the new couple. However, leaving space for the new adult partnership to grow may infringe on and impact the benign spaces already created for co-parenting.

5. There are no sweeping generalizations for parents about the best age for separation. This is the *trickiest* factor, because it depends so much on the temperament, resiliency, and birth order of the individual children. Separations when children are young bring more opportunities for the benign space to develop and grow. Separations when children are teens may have solid parenting connections to return to in creating the more benign space.

NOW MORE OF THE STORY

What happened next in the rearranging of my family? The children grew and started their own families. The following chapter brings my story up to date. Then, chapters 7 and 8 look at how these factors played out in longer stories of family rearranging. Six heterosexual families are profiled in chapter 7, and six gay and lesbian families in chapter 8. These stories show the sticky, serious, and silly ways that separated parents are kin forever.

6

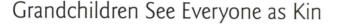

Grandchildren See Everyone as Kin

Our kinship connection endured through remarriage, my second divorce, payment of college tuitions, and watching our kids waitress and bartend as they moved toward their professional identities.

In September 1998, our daughter married. That occasion was my first chance to meet her stepmother's extended family. Remembering many ways they had been kind and generous to my children, I wanted to say thank you in that formal setting. So, 23 years after our separation, I felt real warmth in greeting and toasting my daughter's stepmother's extended family. This large family had loved and been devoted to my children for many years. It was lovely to finally greet them.

On the bride's side of the aisle were many from her stepmother's family, as well as my former in-laws, a large coterie of aunts and uncles and cousins. It was lovely to be in that big circle celebrating the bride and groom but also celebrating how these kinship connections had thrived over the years. In November of that same year, my son's wedding brought the circle together again, a whole new set of connections as kin.

Although I had no continuing connection with my second husband, it has been healing to continue to include my two stepdaughters as kin. I have never stopped thinking of them as my stepchildren. One was at each of the weddings, with her two daughters. When her father's illness and death occurred, in 2006, I was able to be present to her grief and share in memorials with her and for myself. He and I were divorced, and he had remarried, so I was in no way a widow. But, in a deep way, I felt like a widow. It's complicated.

Other family deaths keep opening lots of questions about kinship—roles and connections that are commonplace today but that have none of the traditional norms and codes. Our new family forms outpace our language and familiar codes of conduct. The social rules and roles are fuzzy.

Aging and health problems bring surprising questions to light for the adults and the children of separated parents. In recent years, I've overheard my adult children and their spouses wondering about the care of all of us, parents and stepparents. One family has seven different grandparents to watch as they age and need care. Quite a daunting task for my kids and their children. In other stories, in chapters 7 and 8, you will hear other sad and touching ways that former partners witness growing frailty.

Other family events bring questions. When my sister died, I struggled to know who to notify and include. My former husband had been close to her and was saddened by her illness and death. I wrote letters when his mother was ill and died. Distance prevented me from attending her funeral, but I wanted to acknowledge those early relationships of love and family connection. My kids' father went to visit my mother when she was frail and close to death. When my children and their now-growing families gather to celebrate weddings or mourn deaths in their father's family, I am not there. And he's not there in my family rituals. But we are both talked about and missed. I send the greetings rather than offer my continuing sense of kinship in person. I continue connections with former sisters- and brothers-in-law whenever shared interests or travel makes that possible.

Memories from long ago can pop up at any time. Those of us who have separated as parents have to develop a tolerance for a lack of complete resolution about the relationship. Adults who haven't had children together can walk away from each other in complete ways. Not so for parents. Even if separated parents have no further contact, the connection in memory and through the children is a part of the family history. And a part that may open again around the events and accomplishments in our children's lives. Our culture doesn't help much in learning to make our way when there is no clear resolution, and one has to deal with the complexity and ambiguity of adult life.

There's an incredible vulnerability between former partners/parents. There's history. There's some kind of ease. Body ease and emotional ease. We had learned to make love and witnessed children being born. After a formal separation or divorce, trust rebuilds in more measured and tentative ways. But one can easily bump up against the borders of former intimacy.

A few years back, I happened to visit our son and his family at the same time as my former spouse. No partners, no potential loyalty conflicts, no tensions. We were there together to celebrate a birthday. Just being grandparents together. I found an old ease and satisfaction in knowing that all our energy would be on our son and his wife and their kids. Our son could just be with his birth parents and bask in that attention. It may be a truism that the closer you were and more fun you had in earlier times, the more likely it is that old conflicts will flare. At one point, as the party was ending, my former husband said to me, "Why couldn't you have been this nice when we were married?" Zero to 100 in a second. I was furious. I had thought I had put all that anger and hurt aside. It wasn't nice a lot of the times. The truth is that infertility isn't nice, and abortion isn't nice, and struggling to figure out how to be parents isn't always nice. And nice isn't always part of a vibrant relationship that can contain sadness and anger and disappointment.

Nobody can get under your skin faster than a former lover. When does the kinship as parents take center stage? When do the old conflicts show up? And take over? If you keep a connection, at whatever level, you may slide into that danger zone of conflict. Same old paradox. If you are getting along, then why did you get separated? If you aren't getting along, then you have the anger and loss and hurt. You can get right to the heart of the matter very quickly.

And now, in 2010, he and I continue to know about each other's lives. But we are in each other's lives on fewer and fewer occasions. We hear about each other from our children and now from our grandchildren. We sometimes have to coordinate a visitation plan, just like the old days—only this time moving the grandsons from house to house. Those four boys, who love all their many grandparents, have only the slightest hint of our rich and complex history. They know only the 21st-century version of the lives of all of us.

Recently, my oldest grandson was completing a kindergarten project and asked my daughter, "Who were your big people when you were five years old?" When told that his Mom's big people were me and Papa, he looked at her in surprise and disbelief. And then, thinking she was joking with him, said, "No, really, who were they?" He had no sense at all of his grandparents being together as a unit. He felt loved by each of us. He loved each of us. But not together.

And a littler grandson, building a Lego fire station, very excitedly said, "You know Papa gave me this fire station. I like Papa." When I said that I liked Papa, too, he was equally surprised and said, "You know Papa, too?" How can you explain to a three-year-old that Papa and I were parents together once upon a time? We had to tell our own kids about separation and divorce. Now we tell the story to the next generation in the kinship circle.

Kinship between separated parents is easiest to grasp when a new child comes into the family circle. That child might be adopted, biological, or step. Children make everyone kin. In-laws feel new connections, stepparents feel new connections. We make a new relationship with each child and watch as all the other adults make their own unique connections. That allows us to feel a sense of building something bigger, something that is both continuous and new. And to find new ways to trust each other.

The weaving in and out of each other's lives continues.

When all is said and done, I feel a deep sense of accomplishment and relief that I could stop being a critical wife in front of my kids. I found a way to have the space to learn about how to walk away from the old hurts and disappointments, to find ways to walk toward being a better mother. There are lots of factors in how we behave with a former partner/parent, but it does ultimately become a series of big and little choices for each of us. We walked away from the chance to raise our children together. But we ended up being good enough parents—apart.

7

Stories of Six Families Recognizing Moments of Kinship

Recognizing kinship may come in one moment. Or it may simply build with time. Parents may recognize their kinship when they first talk of separation. Or they may understand when the first grandchild arrives. This chapter gives a fuller look at the untangling and rearranging in six families and when they recognized their kinship.

As I've interviewed people and put these stories on paper, I've thought many times about family history. As many of you may remember, children in elementary school are commonly asked to do a family project, beginning with drawing a picture of their family. Who's your mother? Who's your father? Where were you born? How many brothers and sisters do you have? Can you bring a picture of your grandmother? I keep wondering what the little second-graders born into these rearranged families will write. How will their grown-ups help them to tell the story of their place in these big families? And how will the teachers react to and respect the connections described in words and shown in photos?

The six families profiled in this chapter represent a variety of family circumstances, both positive and negative. Families with young children, families with teens, families in which there were no new adult partnerships, and families in which new adult partnerships had important impacts. Families that stayed in the same neighborhood. And families that rearranged across an ocean.

NAN'S STORY

Nan and Carl were married in 1970, separated in 1985, and divorced in 2000. I interviewed Nan in 2008.

Nan and Carl's marriage oozed apart for many years. They formally separated in 1985, when their children were quite young (3, 7, and 11). They continued to live in the same community outside Boston. They each dated, but dating went on outside their strong commitment as parents. They were one of the couples who separated but stayed legally married for another 15 years. Their decision to legally divorce was made in 2000, when the children were well into adulthood. By that time, they had a well-established kinship circle around their children. They celebrate holidays and birthdays together with a large extended family. There was no question that they considered each other kin.

Carl remarried in 2002, jolting the established kinship circle. His new partner found it difficult to live with the continuing close relationship between the parents. Joint family celebrations with children and joint celebrations with Nan's extended family ended. Carl and his new wife established much more separate lives. Many new couples ask for this stronger, clearer, more separate boundary.[1] New stepparents have trouble enough finding their place with stepchildren. It may be just too daunting to wrap their hearts and minds around extended kinship connections early in the game. New couples need space and time to establish their own traditions. This means another period of rearranging for everyone. The thicker, clearer boundaries of the new relationship may soften and open as time goes by.

As you will see, a medical emergency brought further rearranging for this family. A whole new boundary of kinship was in place by 2007. The boundaries and connections in this family continue to grow and change.

The Beginning

Nan and Carl were both in grad school in 1969 and noticed each other from a distance. An unexpected meeting revealed earlier crushes on each other. "When we began to date, it was never casual."

Their life together as married grad students began in 1970. When their first child was born, Nan decided to give up her studies to become the primary breadwinner. Their tiny apartment grew crowded as a second baby came along. No longer the free and easy grad school couple, they moved to a larger house and, by 1982, had three children, felt emotionally dissatisfied with their marriage, and were burdened by financial stresses. "There were a lot of complicated things about career choices. We had little income because he was working on his dissertation, and he wasn't making much progress. He just wouldn't start writing the dissertation.

"I was the breadwinner. My father was actually giving us money on a monthly basis. When our second child was born in 1978, I insisted that Carl had to do something to get some money. He started a part-time job and did part of the childcare, more than I did during the week. Then, on the weekends, I did most of the childcare."

The childcare and housework decisions were mightily influenced by the women's movement. Loud and long discussions ensued all over the country as couples forged a new way to take care of daily life.[2] "Part of the women's movement was that tough stance about childcare and housework. The mantra was: We have a kid, and you're doing 50 percent of the childcare. I'm not doing it all and cooking and doing all kinds of housework."

These strains about childcare and money were not out of the ordinary in their social circles. "Every family we knew was double professionals. We were all in the same boat, the same struggles about money and childcare and housework. And, I was struggling with having dropped out of grad school and feeling like a failure."

Nan's paid work was in the antiwar movement of the early '70s, a time of big feelings and big causes. A colleague caught her attention, another crush, and she became emotionally involved in a big way. "I fell in love with somebody else. I never had a physical relationship with him. I actually tried, but it didn't happen. It was somebody I worked with who was involved in a really messy divorce. I found myself in the role of confidante and healer for him. I found his neediness to be an incredible aphrodisiac. I don't know any other way to put it. Anyway, I fell in love with him, and my husband knew it. He observed a good deal of it. We even talked about it."

Therapy

Talking was an important part of this couple's life together. Their connection on an intellectual level of understanding was never broken. "One of the things we tried was couples therapy with a therapist who I would love to sue for malpractice." They went to several appointments together, but then the therapist decided to meet with each partner individually. "In retrospect I think that she kind of validated each of our senses of grievance toward the other. That may not have been her intention, but that's what happened. So, rather than communicate why we had been in love with each other in the first place and what we needed to do to feel more connected, she helped each of us feel sort of self-righteously aggrieved.

"For a year, we each met alone with her. It really divided us. We had no previous experience with therapy, and we didn't have any standard to judge it by. We were struggling with the fact that we had three children. We were struggling with the pain that we were causing each other. We would have these fights and then we would have our therapy separately, no place to talk together. I would come home and weep every time."

Formal Separation

After a year of therapy and unceasing unhappiness, Carl started sleeping in another room. This is a fairly common decision in marriages that ooze apart. Nan found this intolerable. She recalls overhearing her son tell someone that his father slept in the living room "as if it was a normal thing. After that I said, 'I can't stand this. Go if you're going.' He left. We just had that one separation by mutual consent. It was painful, but there weren't high dramatics and fireworks. He thought that I wanted him gone, and I think that that's probably true. In retrospect, I think that I was the one who did more clearly want out. I really pushed him out the door. Maybe by sleeping in the living room, he was trying to say, 'Please beg me to come back.' I don't know. We never could get clear about how to talk about the pain.

"At the time we physically separated, the children were 3, 7, and 11. We told them about the separation together. We sat them down and told them. I remember it was my daughter's birthday. We got through the party and then told the kids. I have always felt bad about that, that her birthday is a reminder of the separation. We tried to tell them that we were making each other unhappy, not that somebody did a bad thing. We had no models in the family for divorce—none."

Models

Even though this couple's experience fit into the huge wave of divorce that reached its peak in 1981,[3] they were not aware of their part in a larger cultural and social movement. "Divorce really tore the neighborhood apart, as well as tore families apart. In one family, the father left and the kids were either gone some of the time or all of the time, and those were my kids' friends. They weren't all here at the same time anymore. Family schedules weren't synchronized. This is an unexpected consequence of separation—the neighborhood, not only the families. It was less of a neighborhood because of the divorces.

"Almost everybody that we knew was shocked when they heard we were separating. There were other families that we did joint things with—camping and Sunday morning brunches. They were shocked. Our friends thought they knew us. They thought that we were so solid and so committed to our kids." And the friends were not wrong in seeing their commitment to kids. This couple had already established that space of benign emotional energy between them, the space for caregiving for children. "We did do everything as a family, but our friends didn't know how unhappy we were as a couple."

Rearranging

Carl moved from sleeping in the living room to sleeping in a new apartment. The couple decided to keep the children in the family house and to continue to move in and out. They had long ago established a schedule that was working for the two busy, alienated parents. Certain days of childcare were Carl's, and certain days were Nan's.[4] The parents simply continued their plan in the early part of their untangling. "I stayed in the house in the neighborhood. My father had helped us buy the house so, for the short term, I stayed. We weren't sure it was going to be long term or not. He moved to a really crummy place.

He was not willing to let the kids come to that place, so the only place he could see the kids was at the house. Two or three afternoons a week, I would go away and he would come in. I would wander around after work and then come home when the kids were already in bed. He wouldn't spend the night."

This kind of "nesting" arrangement is a common choice for parents with young children. It usually is very short term as parents realize the need for more space to rearrange their adult lives.

"I found that sharing the house was really hard. I pushed for some better way to do this. He actually moved to an apartment in the building where we had lived when the kids were little. So, after about a year, the kids would go there Tuesday nights and Thursday nights and one weekend a month. They were going back and forth all the time. My youngest daughter, who was four at the time, said, 'This is making me dizzy. I don't know where I live.' So we changed it to half-weeks with me and half-weeks with him. We were switching on either Saturday afternoon or Sunday morning, and gradually we realized that it made the weekends too cut up. You always had to hurry back from whatever weekend thing you were doing right in the middle of a Saturday or a Sunday. So we agreed to do a switch on either Friday afternoon or Monday. Then we'd have the whole weekend. And after another year we went to the whole week at each house."

All of this experimenting with schedules took several years. It finally reached a workable plan because, as Nan says, "We both tried to pay attention. We mostly were respectful. I remember one time I had taken the kids, with his knowledge, to visit my parents. We came back on a late-night flight. He wanted to pick them up right away, and I just wanted to bring them home to spend the night in their own beds. He came to the airport and accused me of trying to take the children away from him. He even went to see a lawyer to talk about what his options might be. Soon he calmed down and realized I just wanted that one night. He finally figured that out.

"We both went to school functions. He was very involved in the kids' activities and sports and chaperoning. As time went on, we didn't have to do too much negotiating; we just did it. They knew which parent to go to.

"We each ran our own households, and we didn't ask for support for our own households. We would then split things—like sports equipment and ballet lessons. My new job in 1988 gave me health insurance for the kids—and for him. We were still married, so of course he would be covered on my policy."

Housing Decisions

"He eventually moved to a nicer house not too far away. Then the kids preferred to go there. My youngest daughter lived there for a while. She had her room there. As the kids got older, they would announce who they were staying with."

These parents were easy with letting the kids have choices about time and space with each parent. Their styles and interests were not threatened if children chose to move in and out. Their lack of interest in planning out the living arrangements for children is surely what made them shy away from going to the courts and making a formal arrangement for separation and childcare. They did not want professionals suggesting how they and their children should make decisions. This family may seem atypical in the kinds of decisions they left to the children. But, they were courageous to follow their own notions about what was best for their kids.

Extended Family

"His family dropped me as if I'd never been part of them, even though we had joint equal custody. His family was still in the kids' lives, just not in mine.

"My family continued to include him. Up to that point, my sister and I had hosted Christmas, and he always came to that. He had a better house for entertaining and, after our kids were finished with high school, he would often host family gatherings. I was always invited."

Legal Steps

Carl and Nan moved almost seamlessly from their life as grad school students with a baby to this new place of kinship. They shared the responsibilities for their children, provided financial stability, and surrounded themselves with overlapping circles of family. The adult-love relationship had not worked, but these two continued to parent with minimal conflict and mutual respect. They didn't know it at the time, but they were in this growing, invisible cadre of parents who separated, divorced, and learned how to be co-parents in respectful and workable ways.

"We were both absolutely clear, and we made a commitment to each other. We promised our kids that we were not ever going to put them in the middle of a fight between us. And we both loved our kids, and we both knew that the other one loved our kids, and we both knew the other would really care for them." Remember, this couple separated in 1985, and the first laws that supported such parenting arrangements had been enacted only five years earlier in California.[4] These were pioneers.

"We finally legally got divorced in 2000. In 1985, we had gone to see a mediator and actually wrote up a divorce agreement about property and money and the custody arrangements. We wrote down what we were already doing. We'd made the plan work, and we never got around to filing it. We were just lazy in not attending to the legal process and to the money issue in an organized kind of way. I just never wanted to call up the court and make the appointment. I didn't want somebody I didn't know sitting and deciding whether or not we were doing a good job. We were just doing it."

New Partnerships

Both Carl and Nan had dated somewhat seriously but never committed to a relationship in which they lived with a new partner. Entertaining together, the involvement with extended family, and the ease of kids going in and out of their houses felt better without the complications of new live-in relationships.

Then that changed for Carl. He made a commitment to a new partner that involved a plan to live together. Boundaries changed again. New live-in couples have different needs for privacy and space.[1] The new partner moved into his house, and they quickly began a big remodeling project. Carl remodeled not only the house but also the then-current family arrangements. "He decided that, in order to be true to the commitment he had made to her, it was no longer appropriate for me to be present at family events. I think it was mostly her urging. He said it was because of his commitment to her. That it wasn't her idea. That's the piece I don't believe."

Carl was now ready to proceed with the formal divorce. "He may have been dating this new woman around the time we actually did finally do all this legal stuff in 2000. I'm not sure whether the timing was related to her or that he was just ready to do it."

Life had held these parents together in close common purpose for 15 years after they formally separated. This new partnership then moved them apart into less connected lives as the children grew into young adulthood. For a time, the extended family had no gatherings. The children spent less time in their father's home. They had less freedom to choose where and when to be with each parent.

The Next Change in the Family Circle

Nan and Carl and his new wife moved gingerly through the wedding of the oldest child, now a 20-something, and the birth of their first grandchild.

Then Carl had a major heart incident. "He was running in a foot race and collapsed. I learned about it because my son called me. He kept me informed."

Nan was in on the family crisis. As with many family emergencies, the boundaries changed and softened. Carl's new wife was not resisting Nan's presence in their life. "During the time between the first and later heart incident, we became a little bit closer again—he and I and his new wife. We talked a little bit more. When he was at home convalescing, they invited me over to their house. We all talked about the kids and our granddaughter and watching our son become a parent. That was an incredible experience. We talked about how we felt about the new grandchild and about this new health crisis. It was a crisis for all of us. All of us were so very grateful for his recovery the first time."

Then he had a second heart attack. It was a confusing time for Nan. Even though there had been increasing closeness after the first heart attack, she didn't know her place as the situation became more serious. She wanted to be with him in what looked like his final days of life. She reached out to friends and counselors for advice about how to handle this situation. No one knows much about how to handle these parts of life.[5] These kinds of families are new to hospitals and medical professionals. There are no medical, social, or religious codes that help families include a former partner in end-of-life issues. No one knows much about how to honor and respect both current and former adult relationships at the same time. Nan was on much better terms with Carl's new wife, but she had no legal or socially assigned place to be at his side in the hospital. She became anxious and obsessed with the notion that she would never see him again. And finally she heard that Carl was in a coma. "I decided to go to the hospital. I didn't ask permission of anyone. It was strange. My middle daughter went with me to the ICU. I would have preferred she had not. I wanted a private time. I just stood by him and talked for a while and apologized for my part of why it didn't work. I have had no illusion that he heard or knew or had any idea that I was there. But I knew it. And my daughter knew. I think she knew it was something very important." Nan wept as she told me this.

Boundaries of the Kinship Circle

There are no precedents for how to do the things involved with the death of a former partner. Funeral directors, clergy, obituary writers are often bewildered by the presence of a former spouse. "I did go to the memorial service, and it was all about Carl and his new wife and some about our kids. There was only one passing reference to the fact that he had had another wife. The memorial service was really hard. There was talk about the wonderful children, but no acknowledgment that these wonderful children were a product of our relationship and our parenting. I was mentioned in one obituary. The other one didn't mention me at all."

Nan and I spoke just months after Carl died. "I have some pictures of him up, and I talk to him some. I just talk in my head. I have a lot of regrets. Maybe I can regret it now when I can't do anything about it. I don't mean that it is dishonest regret. But regret for what could have been. Certainly as I've grown old, I've cherished more the value of a long relationship and have had greater regret than I had when I was younger.

"I don't really feel like his widow. Something in between. His widow is someone else. I recently filled out a form that included a question about marital status, and I began to think about that. My ex-husband is deceased. For some reason, I think there should be a box for that.

"I had coffee with his widow recently. We're trying to be supportive of each other. It's a little weird. But there's a kind of kinship because we're both grieving the same person. I still feel that I have to tiptoe around and make sure that I'm not walking into a space that's not mine. And I think that might be what was always threatening for her. He and I shared a lot. She never had that history. She can't ever move into the space that is the first wife's and the mother's."

The Future

"There's another wedding coming up and a new baby about to be born. He won't be there. The first grandchild was eight months old when he died. One of the things that makes me cry is to think that he's not living to watch those babies grow up. I just can't get my brain around that. I look at my granddaughter and think she's never going to know her grandfather. That breaks my heart.

"We were good parents. One of the characteristics of our marriage and one of the reasons probably that we didn't save it was that we put such a large portion of our emotional energy into our kids and less energy into us as a couple.

"Now I keep trying to encourage my son and his wife to go out. I offer to babysit so they can spend some time together. I think they're very committed to each other, but I worry that they're not taking enough nurturing time with each other.

"I have a cutting board that was his from before we were married. It's kind of broken and scrunched, but I keep it. That feels good to me. It kind of stands for what we went through. When I look back, I'm glad at the end we were friendly."

Summing Up

Nan and Carl's story is certainly one of oozing apart and riding the waves of staying connected with some distance and some closeness. They continued to be married for 15 years after formal separation. They experienced the disconnection that comes with new relationship choices. At the time of their separation, they had young children, which required them to have a good deal of contact. The space for benign energy grew as they set aside the adult feelings of loss and anger. They had 15 solid years to surround their children with the benign energy.

Although they had financial stresses, they were able to come to terms with sharing resources. "Part of a later issue was how much I owed him for his interest in the house. At some point, I gave him an accounting. I said, 'This is how much I think I owe you. Let me know if you think that's right.' He never did, and I never paid him. Finally, I announced, 'I'll just pay for the third kid's college and hope that offsets what I owed for the house. You never did get back to me about how much I owed.' We didn't care much about money, and we were getting along fine."

Therapy did not work for Nan and Carl as a couple, although therapy was a good choice for them. They both had a basic trust in talking and trying to work things out. The decision of the therapist to see them separately was risky. Maybe they did need the space alone, but it made the space smaller for possible repair of the adult relationship. Their ability to talk, to put feelings into words, and to put the needs of their children in the center of their commitment to each other is clear. Nan is both proud of it and regrets it. "What saved our parenting was what doomed our marriage." They were able to be good parents apart. They were not able, in the '70s and '80s, to work out how to be good parents and lovers at the same time.

VIRGINIA'S STORY

Virginia married in 1978, separated in 1991, and divorced in 1996. I interviewed her in 2007.

This family also oozed apart gradually, but, once separated, the parents divorced quickly. One partner remarried quickly. All three adults learned how to be important to one another and to the children. This kind of family is new—first possible in this late 20th-century time of family change. All three adults continue to live quite close to one another in a suburb of Cleveland.

"So this is the unit that goes forward. We're an extended family, and it's kind of funny because Dan and I used to joke, when we were married, about divorce being the new extended family. You know, aunts and uncles don't live down the street anymore. This three-parent family really works for us. It must have been hard for Joan to enter into a situation like that. I don't know why a young woman would want to. But I'm glad she did."

As Virginia begins to tell her story, she notes, "Dan and I got married in the blizzard. You know, there are two parts of a blizzard. We got married in the middle." Shortly after their children were born, each partner experienced the death of a sibling. "We were in tatters. What happened to us was I realized how closed up Dan was and how unable to cope with emotion and grief. He was lost and unfocused at work and making a lot less money. He was in such bad shape."

Dan needed support. Virginia needed support, too. Neither could give to the other. Many people spoke of intense grief and loss before thoughts of separation began to rumble around. The losses left people in tatters and unable to be present. In some partnerships, emotional resources were drained out of an otherwise strong relationship, while, in others, the punch of grief and loss made the emotional separation obvious. The latter is true for Virginia's story. The blizzard of loss and grief blanketed this couple.

Untangling

Years were spent wandering around each other, stunned by grief and not knowing how to find each other. "There were basically four separations while we were in the house. I was talking about our marriage ending for a long time, and Dan thought I was talking about it for effect, that I didn't really mean it. He didn't understand I was serious. I would make more steps, like finally moving into the guest room and suggesting that he take the kids on separate vacations and things like that.

"We had couples therapy early in the game. He didn't like that experience, because he thought the couples therapist was on my side. Late in the game, we went to another couples therapist. I treated that therapy as a situation where I could help him to see that the marriage was really over. He had chosen this therapist. I think that she understood what I was doing, and it did help to clarify the situation.

"There was a moment when I finally said, 'If you want to stay with me, you have to be crazy. I've been telling you for a long time that this relationship isn't working for me. It's not a relationship that can possibly make you happy if it's so bad for me.' Somehow I put it in such a way that he got it. He finally agreed that he would move out. Making this physical separation took really about three years to happen."

Rearranging

At the time of separation, many people expect to feel relieved. They are surprised to feel many other things: anger at themselves, or their partner, or the universe. "I felt sad and tense and guilty. Me! I felt very guilty." Many feel guilty about having taken their own needs seriously or taken action. Many feel guilty about having broken marriage vows or gone against the expectations of the culture.

"We told the kids together. It was horrible. I still can't even think about it without my stomach lurching. We sat down in the kitchen with the kids. We had it all planned. I wanted to communicate to the kids that we were still going to be a family. We're going to be a different kind of family. All the usual stuff—this is not your fault, this has nothing to do with you. We still love you. And, Dad and I still care about each other. We just don't feel like we can live together. The kids simply said, 'You don't fight that much.' They had an idea that divorce was about fighting. We did fight. It was fairly obvious that we weren't happy. We were staying in separate rooms. We were going on separate vacations. But they'd had some friends whose parents had had pretty awful divorces that year. They saw their friends having to choose between their parents and things that were very messy. That's why they asked about that."

She remembers wishing that the kids would understand more about divorce and fighting. But kids can never understand adult troubles. They're kids. There was the sadness because she could not make sense of this for her children.

"Dan then began to think about plans for himself. He had always been very, very dependent on me. When he moved, he actually had me come and look at the apartment. I went and bought sheets and things for the kids' beds. We did it collaboratively."

Schools Begin to Tackle Divorce

As the number of separations and divorces rose during the '80s and early '90s, public schools began to develop programs for kids. Sometimes the programs helped, but sometimes not. The adults in schools were fumbling to catch up with the wave of family change.

"It just so happened that that very year, when we were separating, the guidance counselor at school was setting up a divorce group for the sixth-grade class.[6] My son was put into the divorce group right as this was happening. It turned out to be really awful for him. On the first day, the leaders went around the group and everybody told how long their parents had been divorced. He felt really foolish when he said, 'Two days.' It was so new. He was still in shock. I think the group probably was good because he didn't feel like he was alone. But he was the one who absorbed the pain of it. And he had to face all this as a preadolescent."

The daughter in this family was in second grade. "She didn't really have as much trouble with it at all. At that point, none of her friends' parents were divorced, but then boom, boom, boom, the divorces started. In fact, the very next year, she got a phone call from her best friend saying that her parents were getting divorced. She came to me heatedly and said, 'Mommy, Mommy, Molly's parents are getting divorced. I've got to go to her immediately.' So we drove over. The school noted all the divorces in the early grades and started a group for those girls. The girls continued to be very close, all the way through high school. I think they got a lot out of it. And I don't know too much about what happened, because they took confidentiality very seriously."

Kids have such differing responses to parental separation. In this family, there was gender difference, an age difference, and a difference in the kinds of peer support that developed. The kids were young enough to have years to live with their parents and a new partner and to learn how to live in the extended family. But, as Virginia says, her oldest boy absorbed the pain of it. Maybe that was his temperament; maybe it reflected other factors. It is such a confusing puzzle to understand kids and divorce. Even when kids are grown, putting the pieces together to understand the impact of parental untangling and rearranging can be hard. What is true is that, as adults, we all have the opportunity to make sense of our growing-up years, whatever happened. It's not the exclusive province of kids whose parents have separated.

Formal Separation

"We went to a mediator for the separation. We got an agreement and stuck by it. I stayed in the house. I don't know how I did it, if you want to know the truth. I took care of the house with just the child support money. It was a huge house. Finally, I got a bunch of tenants on the third floor. That was difficult. That whole era was a bit of a nightmare for me."

She had wanted the separation but had not planned for the resources necessary for her part of the two household arrangements. She still struggles with resources for herself.

The logistics of parenting were not a problem. The parents lived quite close to each other and had a regular schedule for the children of visits every other weekend and every Tuesday night. "He'd go to things at school and games. He took them on school vacations. They could walk back and forth between my house and his apartment.

"It was pretty civil. I'm not very rigid about anything in particular. I was the lead and took care of all the doctors' appointments and clothes and food. He's kind of disorganized about those things, but he's a good man and he definitely has a good heart. I didn't mistrust him in any way."

Rearranging Begins

"He started dating really fast. He was a guy who was intent on getting married. The first indication that he was dating was when my daughter's friend called and said, 'Your Dad's kissing some woman in front of the movies!' She rushed to tell me about it. I don't know if she told her Dad. That relationship didn't last.

"The next person we heard about is the person he did marry. She turned up in the first year and a half that we were divorced. And I think he's really happy with her. Joan's perfect for him. And the children have good relationships with her."

The children grew through elementary school and high school in this new configuration of family. Adults and children were witness to the birth of their father's third child, his first in the new partnership. "They have a child, a seven-year-old right now. It was extremely exciting to be part of his birth. My ex's new partner had to have in vitro fertilization. I was kept apprised of the number of eggs that were implanted at any given time. So we've really had a lot of time together. The three of us, you know, it's a relationship. I like her.

"When the new baby was born, it was a big deal. My daughter took the call. She was so excited and wanted to go to the hospital. She said, 'Mommy, would you take me?' I was confused. I thought it would be very awkward. But she really wanted to go. So I said, 'What the heck.' I went with her. And it was wonderful, and it didn't seem to be a big problem. Then my son came home from school later that night, and he wanted me to go with him. He was older and could drive, but I thought it might be a little too much for him all alone. He really wanted me to go with him. I felt a little funny, but I did it. I went to support my son, but it really was such a connecting bridge for me, going that second time.

"Now there's a real bond between that baby and me. My daughter was listening as Joan was putting him to bed one night. Joan was telling him all the people who loved him. I was definitely one of the names on that list. That's really nice. He comes to my house, and we have routines. I have a drawer for him with all kinds of art supplies and stuff. I babysit for him. Sometimes, Dan and I do the planning, but recently we're trying to establish an e-mail exchange so I can coordinate with Joan directly."

The Extended Family

"We spend Thanksgiving and one night of the Passover Seders together. In recent years, we've done Rosh Hashanah, too. I usually have the meal to end the fast. We do holidays and birthdays for the kids together. When his family comes into town for holidays, some of them stay with me. We're family."

They have found a way to keep family history and to have family connections that are useful. No one is trying to remake the original couple connections. They are realistically placing themselves within the kinship circle.

"When Dan and I meet, we don't hug. Greetings are from a distance. It's interesting, because I hug everybody else. I hug Joan. I think she really appreciates me. She thanked me for making it so easy.

"In 10 years, I expect to be at their son's graduation, still celebrating with the whole extended family. I'm also pretty sure I'll be involved when my ex's mother dies, because she's my kids' only grandparent. They never had any other grandparent."

Deep Satisfaction

"I am very proud of this, but I don't give it much thought until somebody says something. They usually say, 'Oh, this is unusual.' But it's not unusual for me. My parents were divorced. I had negative models for marriage and family. I'm just glad that there's somebody around to be family—for me and for my kids."

There's still a great deal of fluidity between these former partners and the new three-parent unit.

"Anytime he wants something, he can come over and get it. We had some nice art, and that was divided. That was easy. He got what he wanted, and I got what I wanted. I'm still a little upset because I can't find the children's books. And I think they must be in his basement. That upsets me. I really wanted to save them. I loved those books. But, I won't go clean up his basement—never, ever. I'll give up the books first. So I hope we're going to find them."

Long-term Money Issues

"The money is the most unsettling part for me. I don't think it worked out well for me money-wise. After we separated and had an agreement, he bounced back from his grief and was more focused at work. He made a lot more money. The agreement was already written and signed. I didn't revisit the money or think about revising the separation agreement. He's been generous, but I have a feeling that if I'd had a lawyer I would have gotten a lot more money. And I'm now facing retirement without enough money and I'm feeling like, oh, I don't know—what a price, what a price!

"I supported the house myself and then sold it and gave him half of the sale price. That was not a good idea. I think that my guilt was playing out here, too. I think there might have been a way to figure it out differently, but I just couldn't think it through. If I was going to be supporting the house, I should have had more help with it, with dealing with it. He didn't offer to help then, but after the child support payments stopped, he took over the health insurance payments for me."

Kinship

This family is an example of recognizing kinship early and easily. As these parents rearranged their relationship to each other and added a new family member, there were changing circles around their two children and the new baby. Separated parents each have an investment in their child, and they will be around forever. In this family, there was an investment in a new child, important to everyone in the family but related in such differing ways. Separated parents can come to look at each other as someone to care about in a new way, because they form the family in which all the children are at the center.

KEN'S STORY

Ken is a retired professor living just outside Philadelphia. He and his former partner married when they were in their late 30s and so were eager to have children right away. They married in 1967, had two daughters, and separated in 1984. Their divorce was final the next year. I interviewed Ken in 2006.

He is proud to tell me that he and his former wife still "date" after a separation of 26 years. However, as cordial as they are today, Ken says, "We were apart right from the beginning of the marriage. Even on the honeymoon, every bump in the road was difficult. It was a kind of a continuous eroding process with little jumps along the way. We would have good times together. We did have a good family life. We went lots of places together. We went to the beach. We went skiing together. We spent a year in Germany when the kids were little. We had all those nice things together but always with that underlying disconnection.

"And then we'd have periods of intense alienation. I would be driving home from work, and I'd find myself asking, 'Are June and I having a fight today or not? Or was that yesterday I'm thinking about?' It was always so tense."

Untangling

"We did have some family therapy. I think we sabotaged the efforts of every therapist. June and I criticized the therapists and what they did. It was not a very good situation. We really didn't use the therapy." Family therapy was in its infancy in the '70s. Therapists were struggling to discover what worked to help families.[7] A fair question to ask in this case is whether the therapy was not good or whether this family was not willing to change its patterns. Did the partners not trust the therapist—or did they not trust each other to be vulnerable to change?

"I don't think we ever really talked about divorce. My memory of it is we knew our marriage wasn't going well. We'd say, 'Well, if that's the way it's going to be, we really shouldn't be together.' I know the tension was being manifested upon the kids. They knew all the hostility. The kids have stories of cowering in each other's arms upstairs when we were angry.

"There were times she would go off for a while, in a pique, or I would not be around for long stretches of time, but when we separated it was very spontaneous. When the breakup came, we simply had an argument about something. I wasn't planning to leave, and I don't think she had any plan, either. We had our usual fight, but this time I stomped out and said, 'This is it! I'm getting out of here. This is the end.'

"I do remember my oldest daughter coming out tearfully and saying, 'Don't go, Daddy.' And I said, 'I've got to go.' And I got in the car and drove around a little bit and came back to a place on the other side of the house. There were some trees I could look through. I wanted to see what June was doing, how she was reacting. She was still raking leaves in the yard, nothing very dramatic. I really had had it. I couldn't go back. I went off and got some temporary housing. It was kind of a scruffy place. I didn't even have a blanket or anything. I camped out there for a day or two. Then, I got a better place to live. But I never looked back. It took some time, but from that point on it was one continuous process. Neither one of us looked back."

Creative Legal Choices

"We were on good enough terms to have some kind of talk. I don't remember that either one of us said we ought to give this another try. We never went back to any therapist."

Historically, the finances in this family were well worked out. "When we were together, we had a financial arrangement for the family. We had a common fund. Each of us kept our own checking accounts. She had some money of her own and decided to hire a lawyer—a powerful lawyer. With disdain she told me, 'I've got this lawyer, and he's going to take all your money.' I remember saying, 'I don't have any money. What is he going to take?' She went through her money in no time with that lawyer. We had only one session with him, and it was very confrontational.

"Then I took charge of the process. The university had a service for employees, so I went to them. He charged a decent enough rate and was very agreeable to what we needed. So I went to June and said, 'How does this sound to you? Usually what the divorce has to do with is property and custody. Let's use this university service.'

"In spite of the hostility, we'd already agreed what was to happen to the kids. It made more sense for the kids to stay with June, a woman with female children. I had a good relationship with the kids, and, in many ways, it would not have been a bad idea to take them on. But, I still think, for two preadolescent girls, it was best not to be with a man all the time.

"Once she talked about a restraining order. She brought up some incident when she felt threatened, and I remember the kids saying, 'Mum can get an order against you, but you can come and visit us.' They knew she wasn't making sense.

"We had a house and a cottage at the shore, and we had some general ideas about what we wanted to do about the property. She had gotten over the 'I'm going to take you for all your worth' kick. So we went to our tax accountant, and he mediated. Maybe he touched a little on the family relationships, but mostly it was property. We decided about the houses. There wasn't much savings. So, we went to the accountant and then to my lawyer at the university and directed him to write the agreement. I took the leadership in all this and, to this day, I have never heard from June that it was a mistake to separate."

Rearranging

"I don't know what I thought I was going to do when we separated. I knew I could live alone, and I knew that, one way or another, I was going to maintain a relationship with my two daughters. That was solid. That was immovable.

"We had the necessary division of labor as parents, but June really did take all the crap of adolescence. In some cases, she didn't do quite what she could have, but I'm not sure she would have done any more if I had been there. For better or worse, she had to put up with a lot. The drinking, the dating, all that kind of stuff. I didn't have to decide how late the girls stayed out or where they were because June was there. I did have a lot of connection with the kids. I was doing a lot of food preparation, a lot of transporting, a lot of discussing and mentoring. But June had the day-to-day."

New Partnerships

Neither one of these adults has gone on to form a new partnership. Ken's given his singleness a lot of thought. "I've been a dater and an isolate all my life. Sometimes, people fix me up, and I have a date. Sometimes I feel alone but, generally speaking, I don't have any deep sense of loneliness. Whenever

I begin to feel alone, I think of how much better off I am than when I was in that marriage. Then, it was the absolute frustration and anxiety and depression about being in an insoluble situation. That was so miserable. I think a few minutes of loneliness is a fair trade-off."

Extended Family and Friends

"Telling family and friends was not overly difficult. June's mother had died. June was alienated from her father. My father had died. My mother was around. My mother's health began to fail some years after the separation. She was pretty sick and always rejected medical intervention. June was a big help to her, because June had worked in a hospital situation and had ideas about how to help. And my mother would listen to her.

"Friends weren't much of an issue. Some were okay with the separation, but some people are still very uncomfortable when we do things together. We have a pretty good time when we're in social situations. We tease each other, and we make jokes about our marriage. And other people don't know what to do with that.

"We have come closer together over the years. In the divorce and right after the divorce, the lines were more firm. She, in particular, was reluctant to do the things that would put us together.

"Now we celebrate family events together. We just did Easter, we always do Christmas. Birthdays, too. She calls me sometimes just to talk about things that are bugging her in her life and her work. I'm a sounding board for her. Sometimes, she calls and says, 'I've got some heavy thing to put into the garage. Would you come over?' But, after I help, I might hear, 'There are a few things the matter with your character which I'd like to call to your attention because they drive me crazy.' It's still confusing for us. We can bump up against that hostility pretty quickly. The edge is always potentially there.

"Occasionally, we date. For her Christmas present, I took her out to a very nice show and dinner. We'll do a family thing down at the beach house, and I'll say, 'We're going to do the birthday thing for supper, do you want to stay over?' She sometimes does, but I think she has trouble with that. I think it feels too intimate for her." When Ken and June meet and greet, they just say hello. "There's no touching between us."

The Next Generation

"When our first grandchild came along, we drove up together. We talked a lot of good stuff out together. No problem. Seven hours of driving. I drove back again three days later, and June stayed on to help with the baby. She flew back, and I picked her up at the airport. She gave me a little report. After that, we often flew up there together. I do think that out of all of this, the fact that June and I do have this quasi-friendly family relationship, that's terrific."

What's the Right Thing?

"I still have some trouble with the decision to separate. I often think that separating was a selfish gesture. But I remember thinking that the marriage tension was going to kill me. I thought I'd either have a heart attack or become dysfunctional and depressed. I don't have any terror of being alone. If I stayed, I think it would have destroyed me."

Ken wanted his daughters to have better models for living their adult lives. "I'm constantly concerned about whether I did the right thing by the girls. I've usually ended up thinking it wasn't the right thing for the girls, but the alternative wasn't the right thing, either. So, I don't have any magic answer. I don't think I could have done anything much different. I was not growing in that marriage very much. I think that I'm a better person now. And I can be of service to my children. In that marriage, I was more twisted and rigid and frightened. I feel good about who I am to my daughters now."

LIZABETH'S STORY

This is a story of recognizing and protecting kinship in a family that rearranged across the Atlantic Ocean. Lizabeth devoted herself to keeping the kinship ties between father and children. "He was not a very present kind of father—sort of a Peter Pan kind of guy." She wanted him to stay in the picture.

Lizabeth had been living in Spain, studying language and working in Barcelona. When on vacation, she met a young Spanish man, married, and moved to the Catalan countryside to start a family. They married in 1985, separated in 1996, and divorced two years later.

She had been "seeing a therapist" in Barcelona before she met her husband. The notion of finding a family to belong to was strong for her. She wanted a large and loving family, her stereotyped notion about what a Spanish family would be.

"A therapist once asked, 'Did you marry his mother?' I definitely married the family. My own mother died when I was two, and my father remarried when I was four. Then there was a lot of heavy drinking. When my father and stepmother finally got divorced, I was in high school. I know my father leaned on me in a way that was very inappropriate."

She adopted her husband's family and felt comfortable and loved. They had two children rather quickly. As in most marriages, having children puts new strains on what otherwise might have been an easy connection between adults. The conflict and hurtful anger came quickly for Lizabeth and her young husband.

"When things got really strained for us, we went to some therapy together. He had gotten physical with me and angry, not to the extent where I was in the hospital, but very threatening. The anger came into the therapy sessions, and the therapist began to tell me, 'This is untenable.' So I started thinking, I need to leave. I should go to the States. It was almost like a survival instinct, for me to get out and come back home."

She turned to the adopted extended family for some protection in her marriage. "My mother-in-law had a horrible marriage. She did not leave. Her family told her she had to stay. I had been close to an uncle in the family. The uncle had stayed in his difficult marriage, too. I wanted some understanding from him. He couldn't respond when I reached out to him. He basically said, 'Go home, it'll be okay.' The message was definitely to put up with it and stay in your marriage no matter what. I didn't want his family to deny him and support me, but I began to realize that they couldn't support me against him. When the uncle ducked away, I realized, 'Ooh, right, I don't have a family here. This isn't my family.' The realization that I couldn't expect them to give me unconditional support made it very clear that I needed to leave. I knew my support was definitely here in the States."

Untangling

"I had come to the States every summer to see my family and friends, and one summer I decided not to go back because it had gotten so tense and hostile. We were fighting all the time, and therapy wasn't working. It was shocking to make the decision. When I declared that I wasn't coming back, he went crazy and flipped out. It was quite hostile in the beginning, but it was also quite sad because he knew why I left.

"I had to go to the consulate and make an affidavit to say I was not hiding the children. Then we got a separation agreement because he wanted the kids to go to Spain for a visit. I was flipped out that he would pull a fast one if I didn't have all the legal documents in order. The kids were only five and nine. I made him sign a separation agreement before he could take them. Every step required a lot of courage from me.

"They were so little and I was so worried. I was surprised when he saw how distressed I was to let them go. I have to give him credit for seeing that. So, to help me, he said, 'I don't know what it is about mothers and children, but if either kid can't handle this, I'll bring them home. Even if it's you who can't handle it, I'll bring them home.' That changed everything. Then I could let them go."

"We did the divorce between us, and then I hired a lawyer. I was so devoted to being independent and so uncomfortable about talking about money that I didn't press him. I still don't get much child support. In the middle of the divorce, I had inherited a bunch of money, and he had to know about that. I had friends who helped and gave advice, but no friends who had gone through a separation. Everyone always pushed this money question. But I didn't want to poison my life only thinking about money all the time. I didn't push the usual legal battles. I just wanted to be free."

Rearranging

"A big issue was going to be how he was going to spend time with them. I didn't want them going to Spain a lot. I was dedicated to trying not to make anything more cumbersome for him and the kids than necessary. So he would fly to the States and would stay at my house. I would either go somewhere or would work a lot. He would come here, and I would half hold my breath for two weeks. A lot of people thought I was crazy to do that. But I was so guilt ridden that I had left in this dramatic fashion that whatever could be done for him to see the kids was what was important to me. Ultimately, I wanted our kids to have their own relationship with him, because I had to be in the middle so much with my father and stepmother. I think there was empathy for the kids being in that situation. I wanted to handle it better for my kids."

This is not a cozy relationship between separated parents. The vision of family and all the creative work to keep the family connected is done by one parent. Lizabeth did create benign space for her children. "I still balance my need for being unencumbered and not being poisoned by anger and stress with not approving of the way he handles himself. He just wanders in and is a free spirit. So there's no renewed closeness between us as adults. I don't respect him. The driving force for me has always been letting the kids figure out their own relationship with him. To that end, I sacrifice. So a couple of times a year, I help them be together. I wanted no closed door.

"My youngest, my son, was not very aware of our fighting when we were married. He was young. My daughter was always much more aware of what was going on. She witnessed some of the threatening arguments. She would break out into a ball of hives. When I was thinking of staying in the States, I asked her what that would be like for her. I said, 'If you don't think you can handle this, we don't have to stay here.' Although she'd been raised in Spain, my daughter spoke fluent English, but she'd never written English or studied it. One day I came home and found a Queen Anne's lace flower on my bed and a note written in this tragic English. It was so sweet. She wrote, 'A hard decision is like being at the beach and trying to pick out the best rock. I need to be with you wherever you are.' We always had an open, verbal relationship. I don't mean it was always smooth. There were plenty of times when she would rail and freak out, screaming and yelling that I took her away from their father.

"I was in therapy when we got back to the States, and that helped a lot. My therapist was an incredible *forest guide*. She really helped me through all sorts of things. It was absolutely helpful to have a therapist validate the situation for me. That it wasn't my fault. I learned about the whole issue of not explaining him to the children. At first I fell into that trap a lot because of my own childhood. When I was a kid, I was always trying to explain these two incredibly different personalities and patterns. So when I was in therapy, it was almost like behavioral therapy. Learning how not to take responsibility for their relationship with their father. It was really hard, because I was always trying to protect them. Just deciding *not* to explain this whole thing to my kids was so hard. I learned how to help myself, and then I could help them. I think my example of trying to survive was helpful to the kids."

Validating Reality with Grown Kids

"Now my daughter is 21, and I overheard her speaking to her father on the phone the other day. I could tell from the tone of her voice that she was upset, even though she was speaking softly in Spanish. After she got off the phone, she said, 'He's never going to change.' I had always wanted to tell her that, but I've kept my opinions about him to myself. But that day I said, 'Well, you're right. The only thing that is going to change is how you decide to live with him and how you decide to receive his behavior—or reject it. But that's up to you. You can't expect that suddenly he's going to be the father that you want him to be.'

"We have no contact as adults, just as parents. Now that I'm not bound by other obligations, I am able to say he's a curious, interesting guy. But, boy, he doesn't know how to do this relationship thing. We need an excuse to be in touch, and that's the kids. He won't have to stay here after our son finishes high school. I know he likes to stay here. It's a nice place to stay in the summer. Right now, I am doing some work on the garage. I'm horrified that he might think he can come and stay for a long time.

"He'll participate with kids' weddings, and other things. I don't know what he'll do financially, but he'd certainly be with them wholeheartedly. I feel good about what I've given my children."

There are no legal rules or religious rituals to guide adults in shaping their relationship to each other as they separate and divorce and live on into their lives. There were no models for Lizabeth. She managed to make a space for children to have contact with their father. She protects their right to form notions about each parent. And she did this across an ocean.

ELAINE'S STORY

Elaine and Mike were high school sweethearts in Maryland. They moved with each other to New England colleges and then back to Maryland for his graduate school. Their story involved two separations, one when their two children were young, and the final, formal separation when their children had finished high school.

Their marriage was in 1962. Their first, short summer separation was in 1969. They finally separated households in 1981 and divorced in 1984. I spoke with Elaine in 2006.

"We had sex at 13 and all through college, and that was unusual then. I married Mike because of the sexual guilt. That was so stupid." This was how

Elaine viewed her life choices as a young woman. She had grown up with the '50s codes of conduct about sexuality.[8] Sexual activity was very, very private. Of course, all kinds of sexual exploration was going on, but it was hush-hush. Sex was not a topic of conversation. To think one "had to" marry if one had had sexual intercourse was not an unusual way to think in the social context of the 1950s.

After they married, in 1962, Elaine and Mike had two children (a boy and a girl), and the couple moved through a number of towns around Washington, D.C., as Mike continued his graduate studies and internships. Elaine worked and supported the growing family.

Separation

"The moment that I remember is when he left me when the kids were little. He fell in love with a work colleague. Having to tell little kids that their father wasn't going to be there was devastating, absolutely devastating. I remember my daughter crying and my son being quiet. I tried to keep their lives as normal as possible."

The separation would last for a summer. "He was gone all summer. He was camping with this new woman, moving from one campground to another.

"I lost weight. I cried. If I hadn't had those kids to get up and get me going I don't know what it would have been like. I didn't tell too many people that we were separated. Certainly, the neighbor across the street knew. Anybody who watched me knew, because I was losing weight. I was tense.

"His parents kept calling the house. I had to keep talking to them. I told him I wasn't going to cover it up. When I finally told them he had gone, it was even more devastating. I had known them since I was a young girl. They were really like parents to me."

Another Try

"He finally came back." Elaine wanted him to come home but now wonders about that wish. "I think to myself—why weren't you stronger? Why didn't you get angry? Why were you just so devastated? If I could change anything, I would have been stronger about putting limitations on getting back together. I was groveling. 'Please come back, just come back.' It was such personal rejection when he left for another woman." When he returned, they resumed their university lifestyle and decided to "get through this for the kids."

As a consequence of the tenseness between them, Elaine made a decision to take a bigger job that would allow her some travel and some planned separation in the marriage. Her new job, more than two hours away, had some living accommodations. This meant they were separated during the week and together on weekends.

A Longer Untangling/Waiting

"I felt like I was leading a pretty schizophrenic life. I was making decisions at work, being in control in a leadership position, and then I'd go home and I was walking on eggshells around him. He was depressed. I was mixed up and stressed by the marriage and by my work.

"I had a good job. I had recognition for that job. I was flitting around going to various meetings, leading groups, and that was very affirming. But there was a hole in my life. That's when I began dating around during the week."

Mike continued his sexual exploration, as well. "He started the sexual exploration, but then later I made up for it. We played 'switchies' with another couple some weekends.[3] It was Mike's idea at first. It was exciting. Remember those times—everyone was exploring sex."

As time went on, Mike became involved in a more committed relationship. "I learned of his involvement, because he took this new, more serious girlfriend to a soccer game. I was really livid that he'd do that. I was coming back for all the games. I was coming back and forth for the kids. I was exhausted trying to be there for them. Both kids were active in sports. I still can't believe he did that. Another betrayal."

But, through all this stress and tension, "there was this tacit agreement to wait until after high school to split. We were trying to hang on until the kids were out of the house. That was the agreement."

When the kids finished high school, the relationship finally dissolved. "We never had a sit-down discussion with the kids. At least I can't remember one. It just happened. They knew Mike had a new relationship. They knew we were not a couple anymore."

Rearranging

"I have one memory. I was lying on the bed reading, and Mike came barreling into the room and said, 'Is there any chance to make this work? Do you want to go into counseling?' I think what happened was his new lover told him he needed to really try to make it work before she would commit.

"I was already involved with a new relationship that was becoming more serious. I didn't bring this new guy into my life with my kids. But the tension was mounting.

"I had already bought a house near to my work. Mike began pressing me to move permanently. He was getting very antsy to move in with his new woman and end our living together. When I finally made the decision and told the kids I was moving to my other house, it was very quick. We went around and put tags on all the furniture, tags on the stuff we each wanted. Those kinds of negotiations were difficult. Occasionally, there were raised voices. I didn't fight well with him.

"There was more grief in the first separation. But, there was lots of grief then, too, particularly when we had to divide photographs and all that stuff.

That's hard stuff to do. On the day of the move, I pulled a truck up to the front door, put the stuff in, and left. I remember it was really hard for my daughter. She was crying just the way she'd cried when we separated that summer when she was little. I shouldn't have asked her to be there to help. My son never showed. He stayed away. He was silent just like that first separation.

"I moved out one morning, and his new partner moved in that afternoon. He stayed in the house and eventually sold it. I had no financial interest. It was dumb. There wasn't any contesting of it. It was simple. It was over with. I wanted to get out. I was making good money for the time. I walked away with all the debt ($12,000, a lot for that time). The question of my paying alimony came up. I made more money than he did, so the court might have made me pay alimony. I took over the debt in lieu of paying the alimony to him."

Since the kids were involved with college, the questions of where they lived was negotiated between each kid and a parent. The family just fizzled apart. "My son lived with me for a while. He kind of bounced around. My daughter just went on her way, moving from school to school. She was really independent and very angry. I had a hard time having contact with her from the age of 18 through the age of 24. She was angry all the time, angry at both of us."

No Contact

Years went by with no contact between parents. "I felt no need to stay in touch with Mike." They heard about each other through the kids but had no interest or compelling reason to be in touch directly. "Then he called when his father died."

Mike's parents were family to her, not only because they were her in-laws and grandparents to her children but because she had been a preteen when she first knew them and had strong connections independent of Mike. Her own father had died when she was 10, and she and her mother had a very strained relationship. She was ready, as a young teen, to find a new family, and Mike's family became hers. So, there was no question about attending the funeral services.

"I went to his father's funeral and took the kids. His parents were more parents to me than my mother. I drove down with the kids and stayed in a motel. I just couldn't imagine not being part of that. Not just for the kids but for me."

That was the beginning of a softening between these separated parents. They were able to participate in this life event without the old feelings of conflict and betrayal getting in the way of their current grief.

Two years went by with no contact. "And then his mother died. He called to let me know, and I went back again to my hometown. I had remarried, so this time I was with my husband, John. The kids went, too. My former mother-in-law had a church-based funeral, and we all went in together—Mike and his wife, John and I, and the kids. We all sat in the same row. I heard a lot of whispers about that from behind me. It was hometown for both of us, so everyone knew about our divorce, and I guess they were very surprised to see us all together."

After the funeral, everyone stayed on for a few days. "His mother's house had to be cleaned. They were divvying up things. He asked me to come to the house. We'd given his parents lots of things, and he wanted me to have some choices. He wanted the kids to have their choices, too."

Everyone worked together: the separated parents, the new partners, and the kids. "And then, the next day, we all had had enough of the dust and decisions. We went to a comedy movie together."

Renewed Connection

Since that weekend, there has been much more connection between the parents. "We do better on the phone. We can have long phone conversations and catch up. He'll tell me about what happened to certain relatives. We have this long history. His new wife doesn't have that history with him. We went to high school, for goodness sake. He'll bring me up to date on high school reunions and friends."

They don't spend a lot of time together. But celebrations of life events and rituals around children are now possible. They have left the old, hot feelings behind. They have found the benign space of connections. "My daughter finally got her college degree, and there was a party at her father's house. I took something to the party. There was some tenseness at first, but it was okay. We didn't interact much with each other, but his wife and I got along very well. I tried to be helpful in the kitchen. I think I would really like her. She's an interesting woman."

Ages of Children

This is a couple who "stayed together for the kids." There were long, long years of tensions for both the adults and the kids.

"The surprise about the divorce was that it was very freeing." It is an interesting question as to whether that freeing could have happened earlier if the adults had been able to evaluate more realistically the impact of so much tension on everyone. But what kept these parents together "for the sake of the kids" was probably what made them feel compelled to marry after they had sex as teens. They felt the pressure of what they considered the cultural conventions. "Do the right thing." And getting married if you'd had sex was the convention of the '50s for these white, middle-class kids. Staying for the kids was another convention around them.

Separated parents make decisions within their particular social and historical context. These two adults were trying to make sense of their lives and their impulses in a time of incredible upheaval and cultural change. The pioneers in family change often found paths that dead-ended. Then they turned around and looked for a road wide enough to contain the kinship connections.

SAM, ALEX, AND ERIKA'S STORIES

I was fortunate to have been able to interview a pair of separated parents—Sam and Alex—and Sam's new partner, Erika, in 2006. I interviewed them separately, so the story becomes interestingly woven and challenging. It is not a single story but three separate stories. Their stories point to the ways that separated parents experience new possibilities for connection after the first 10 years. After 10 years, most of the court-ordered connections about custody, visitation, and money are completed or are more or less routine. The heat has been turned down on the power struggles. By then, parents begin to feel freer to participate in relationships with each other by choice and are often able to regain empathy and trust with each other. When separated parents and their new partners see that each is able to be devoted and constant for the children, the remaining hurt and anger and feelings of abandonment are held more gently. After a 10-year period, separated parents who have continued to care for their children see each other in softer ways—feeling respectful, albeit distant. Trust is more measured, more pragmatic, and more fragile.

The Beginning of One Family: Sam and Alex

Sam and Alex met in a commune and gradually came to be lovers. "We were friends at first." They married in 1974, separated in 1995, and divorced in 1998. They lived in and around San Francisco.

They had a long struggle toward separation—from "I can't do divorce" to "I can't do this marriage anymore!"

Alex said, "We had been in couples therapy for about six years. When we left, things had gotten better for about a year and a half. Then everything deteriorated again. We had an in-house separation. At least one summer, Sam didn't want to go on vacation with me and rented a place by himself."

She marked the progress of their oozing apart by the summers, because their two sons went to camps for many weeks, leaving Sam and Alex with the debilitating tension of their relationship. "Nineteen ninety-two was not a good summer. We weren't getting along. The following summer, he rented a house by himself. The next summer, we slept in separate bedrooms when the kids weren't there."

Sam says, "I was dead in the marriage. I was very sick, and when I recognized that I was getting sicker, well, I had no choice. I was between a rock and a hard place—total frustration. I didn't want to leave, but I was not going to get better."

Children held them together. They worked together for their son's Bar Mitzvah, and both agreed that it was a wonderful celebration. "We really pulled together as a family and said some really loving and true things to our son."

The Moment

Shortly after that important family event, they went for a walk. Alex remembers saying she couldn't stand the tension. "If this is what it's going to be like, I can't do it anymore." Sam wanted separation originally but still felt very conflicted about the reality of a separation.

"The decision to separate took a long time. I'm pretty sure it was in the fall. At the time, Alex didn't want it. There was no one else involved. I was feeling sicker and sicker. My body was giving out. One day, I said I definitely wanted a separation. Then she shocked me. She got a lawyer right away. When she told me she'd gotten a lawyer, I said, 'Whoa! Whoa! Whoa! I didn't mean it. Can't I take it back?' I was shattered. We agreed to tell the kids after Thanksgiving."

"Telling the children was one of the hardest things." Alex sighed, "You have to explain to older kids. We decided in the beginning of November. We told the kids the Friday after Thanksgiving." The children reacted differently. "Our oldest started crying right away and said, 'You mean there's going to be no more family vacations?' We did have wonderful vacations. Our younger son went numb. He had feelings about six months later."

Sam still finds it difficult to talk about the experience some 15 years later. "I can't even talk about it. It's just too much," he says through his tears.

Separation as Shredding

Sam says, "My memory is that the relationship got dramatically worse after the separation. It stayed bad until we got the legal divorce three years later. I had the image of being in a shredder, like being fed into a wood chipper, coming apart. I had nightmares about the divorce. I was not feeling relieved to be separating. I was going into the darkness. I was scared.

"Looking back on it, I don't know how I did it. Everything was taken apart. Now that I'm on the other side, I look back, and I am not the same person. I did a lot of body work and psychotherapy to heal."

Alex remembers, "I had hoped to get away from the pain. I did get away from some pain. But new pain came. First there was the pain of living together married, then the pain of telling the kids.

"I was tense, angry, and embattled at first. I was so mad that I didn't do the politically correct thing. I played victim. I was blaming him for wanting the separation. I kept the stance of 'Well, how could you be doing this? Look what's going on. Why don't you look at yourself?' I was just mad and not really saying, 'I love you. I'm sorry for what I've done to you, my part of it.' I was still so mad I was using the role of victim."

The victim role is so common. Someone gets it or takes it.

"And I don't know how you make that victim stuff even, because it isn't. It's probably better to know that both people wanted it. But I know I was confused. Because, yes, I wanted it, but I also was emotionally feeling left, and I was not the one who had wanted it at first.

"It's true I had been the first one to say the words out loud, but I wasn't strong enough to own it. It must have been crazy-making for Sam, because he was the one who was pulling away more, but I had been the one to say I want this to be over.

"And then visitation was so painful. The first night the kids were at Sam's and not with me, I thought I would die. I felt something ripped out of me. I was on the phone just crying to my friends. I sort of let it rip. One reason other people saw me as victim was because I was so emotional."

Drawn-out Legal Negotiations

Alex and Sam had a very long process of untangling. These two parents had a mini-version of the stuck-like-Velcro separation. The struggle was never about custody or visitation. It was about money.

Alex continues, "I had no expectation about divorce, but we went to a mediator. The first thing the mediator said was, 'What I do is talk with people about what divorce really is.' He painted a very difficult picture. I came away thinking, this is too painful. I'm not doing this.

"Then we tried a lawyer. He was an old friend and really litigious. He and Sam didn't get along. This lawyer/friend wanted to save me. After two years of attempts at negotiation, the lawyer said, "Go to someone who will help you get through this. Go to someone who will file and go to court.' Then we found a new mediator and two lawyers. Ultimately, we had a four-hour, four-way meeting in court."

Sam remembers, "Custody issues were not written down. I don't remember ever not being able to talk about the kids. That was just unquestionable. We put the anger aside. Otherwise, we couldn't talk to each other. It wasn't cozy. It was civil. The hard issue was alimony and other money things."

Alex had stayed at home for most of their marriage, with a part-time job and graduate school work. She was just finished with school but did not have her professional license at the time of the separation. She worried about money and, at the same time, hated the idea of taking money from Sam. Sam had said no to alimony.

"The wisest thing I did was go to a financial person who helped me learn about money. I didn't want money from him, but I had never worked full-time. Negotiations were all about money. It was the thing that held up the divorce. We decided to revisit alimony after the child support was done, when the kids were through with college."

Family and Friends

In terms of contentiousness, family and friends came second to the money issues. This couple had a wide circle of friends, and their family connections were close and overlapping. Alex was quite close to Sam's brother and the brother's wife. They knew everything that was going on. They called and stayed very much in touch with her. Alex was quite close to Sam's mother, as well, and had been throughout their marriage. Because of the conflicted nature of relationships in her family, Alex felt like a daughter to Sam's mom. "It was really awful to tell her. She was really supportive to me. Staying close with his mother and brother felt right, but also uncomfortable and unusual. I have a little guilt about that."

Alex had had a troubling relationship with her own mother for many years. There had been some repair by the time of the separation. When she finally told her mother about the separation, "My mother said one of the nicest things she'd ever said to me. It was in her tone, too, not just the words. She said, 'I know you tried as hard as you could.' She died three months later.

"My family turned their back on him. My sister really divorced Sam. My cousin divorced him, too, and told him he couldn't come to Thanksgiving."

Many find it difficult to come to terms with the changed relationships with former in-laws, especially with sisters- and brothers-in-law who may have formed a part of the family's social network. It often takes time to sort out who can remain connected. It is ideal if only the parents get divorced. But often family and friends are drawn in unexpectedly.

Some in their network of friends took sides, too. According to Alex, "I don't think he got as much support as I did. I was so much more emotional and played that victim card. My friends were really angry at him. Sam would get angry back, and then things would be worse. One couple didn't take sides. Some people stayed close to both of us. I'm so grateful for that now."

Sam's memories are very bitter about the friendship circle. "Second to having to tell the children was how hard it was to tell friends. I don't know if any friends chose me. They were mad at me. Their anger was huge and hurtful for me. For years, friends refused to come to my gatherings. They'd say, 'I can't come because of my friendship with Alex.' One of our dearest friends had divorced the year before we separated. I had been so supportive of this woman, so supportive. She was a dear, dear friend. And when it came to be my time to need support, she just walked away. I just saw her a year ago (14 years later), and I said, 'I can't believe you treated me so badly.' 'Well,' she said, 'I was angry because of the way you separated.' I thought, 'What do you know about the way I separated.' That's a grudge I hold toward Alex, making it seem like it was all my fault. And this friend believed her."

Alex had a diagnosis of cancer in the year before the divorce was final. "His mother came to help. I know he felt on the outside. I got my help from lots of other people, a lot of friends that had been his friends, too. He did come to see me in the hospital. I remember he came up to the side of the bed. Everybody left us alone. I had a total blackout, and I don't remember what he said. He probably said some very sweet things, and I just spaced out. I remember he came right up close."

Sam remembers the hospitalization, too. "It was hard when she was sick. The friends again! They were around her and they were still angry at me, so I felt kept away. I couldn't believe that they couldn't understand that I'd have feelings about her, too."

Just recently, Sam and Alex were together at the funeral of her sister's husband. It was the first time that Sam had been with her extended family in some years. "We just went through a funeral, so there was some healing in that. It was nice that she let me know when her brother-in-law died. I gave her a big hug at the funeral, with no hesitation. It was very healing to have several days together. So right now I'm feeling better than I have for some time. It's been so many years."

Alex recalls the family funeral, "I felt very sisterly/brotherly with Sam. I was very sad. It brought me back to being friends with him. We should have stayed just friends. We really should have. We had a great life as a married couple, and we did wonderful things. But we made better friends than lovers."

Today, Alex sees the relationship as "softer, distant. I don't know if distant is the word, but we keep a distance—not in a negative way, in a protective way. I would say respectful and caring, sort of an unexpressed caring."

As Sam talks about their connection these days, he says, "We're friendly now. I wouldn't say we're close. You know, in a very strange way, I love Alex. I still love her. But I'm not comfortable with her. I can hug her now. The hugs came after about five years. Touching now is filled with old body memories. To me, it's not so much the body memories of being lovers, but the body memories of being pushed away by her."

Now that Alex and Sam's children are grown and Sam has a new committed relationship, they are rearranging again. What the family looks like and who is included used to be easier. Now there are three players who have differing notions of family connection and inclusion.

Erika

Erika's history contributed to and enlarged the kinship connections for all adults in this extended family of Alex and Sam.

Erika married in 1969 and spent some periods of time with her husband's family in Brazil. Erika and her husband had two daughters and, in San Francisco, ran a successful family business together. They lived an on-again, off-again separation because they had demanding business obligations, traveled a lot to South America, and had two homes to maintain.

"When I met him, he seemed so sweet, and he was from a different culture. I was swept off my feet. But when he was a husband and a father, he was more like his own father, a military man who ruled the family with an iron hand. He was so perfectionistic. I couldn't do anything right. I always felt criticized."

For many years, Erika had an ongoing internal debate about whether to leave or stay. "I probably wanted out of the marriage a good 15 years before I did it. We were married 23 years before we separated. It took about seven years to get divorced."

"I think what happened was that my physical body started to speak up. I had a physical reaction when I was in the room alone with him. I had a physical reaction of fear, and it was as if I were physically abused. I felt my body tense and on edge. I think my body was just saying, 'I can't take this anymore.'"

After their second child left home, Erika found the courage to act, telling her husband she didn't want to be his wife. "We were in our little den. He was on one sofa, and I was on the other. All of a sudden, I felt physically afraid. I knew I had to act on that visceral reaction."

"I told him I couldn't live being this afraid. It was amazing. He just left, and about three days later called and said, 'Whew, what a relief. Now we know where we stand.'

"For about a year, I was mad. I was angry at him. He was very patient. He kept saying to me, 'I want to be your friend. I don't want to be your enemy. I don't want to be fighting.' And eventually I let go of my anger for all those years of being afraid.

"We went to a mediator. He wanted to make sure I was taken care of. People were shocked that he was so caring. We were not yelling. We talked about having a divorce party to celebrate our divorce, but we never did it. It was just such a relief to feel separate.

"Now he feels like a friend and family to me. Even when we first separated, we never stopped doing family stuff. We'd meet for Thanksgiving or for Christmas, or we'd go out for birthdays. All of his side of the family, you know, they're still my sisters-in-law, my brothers-in-law. I hadn't lost them. I still consider them my family. I will never let go of the family."

Rearranging

She has now been living with a new partner for several years. That new partner is Sam.

After long years of being in a relationship that was oozing apart with tension and fear, Erika found the experience of untangling her former partnership much more congenial than it had been for Sam and Alex. Erika's experience of keeping family ties was also very different. Perhaps it was due to cultural differences. The extended Brazilian family was more inclusive. Perhaps it was the ages of the children. Erika's children were already adults, so there were fewer issues to mediate at the time of the separation. Perhaps it was due to the long experience of having run a business together—or of having the extended separations over many years. In any case, there seemed to be less hurt to heal. Alex and Sam had experienced more fracturing of the family and social fabric around them.

These three adults had big differences in their notions of kinship, differences in how to hold connections/disconnections between former partners and former friendships. How big could the kinship circle get? Who would be included? Who would decide how and when the circle expanded?

Sam and Erika have four children between them, stepsiblings. "All the kids come to visit. They relate very well together. My kids are older. They all seem to understand each other. We have gatherings with my ex-husband here, too, with my kids and with Sam's kids. It seems just fine."

Sam and Alex have had disagreements about how to include Erika in the expanded kinship circle.[9] Alex says, "It was our tradition to go to the airport together to pick up the kids whenever they came home from their travels. Now Erika wants to join in. We never had to negotiate that before. She doesn't have the same boundaries with her ex. She and her ex do a lot together, so it's natural for her to think of being included. But, for me, I just want the two of us with the kids."

In addition to airport pickups, a recent struggle has been about celebrating Passover when kids are home. "Sam came for a few years by himself before he was living with Erika. Now Erika wants to be included. She really is family now. She wrote a letter. I hated the letter. But the letter was helpful."

Erika elaborates, "I was very pleased that a couple of years ago, I was able to go to Passover with my new partner and his ex and the boys. She didn't want me to come at first. At first, he wasn't asked to the Seder, but then she began to include him when the kids were with her. Then one year I said, 'What about me?' And I didn't realize that I had such strong feelings about not being included. I was always so thrilled that she'd invited him. It was so important for him to be with his boys. But that year I really felt left out. I said to myself, 'She needs to know my feelings. She can do whatever she wants, but, for me, I have to tell her my feelings. If I don't tell her, it's going to fester inside me.' So I wrote her a very nice letter and said, 'You know I consider myself Sam's wife. We've been together a long time now. I would like to be part of this. I understand it's your dinner, and you can do what you want. I feel very hurt that I'm not included, and I just want you to know my feelings.' She called up and invited me."

That letter helped to establish a new tradition of all adults being with the boys at Passover and Rosh Hashanah. "But it's still not all that comfortable for me," says Alex. "We are not friends, but we aren't strangers. And we know each other well. I guess we're all learning."

After 11 years, these adults are recognizing their kinship in new ways. Alex speaks about another tradition that is growing. "We always sent each other Mother's and Father's Day cards from the beginning. We respected each other as parents. It wasn't an area of contention. Then, one Mother's Day, he came over with a bouquet of flowers. I was so touched. Maybe he'd noticed how kind Erika and her former partner could be. I think it came from seeing them sharing."

Looking Back and Ahead

"When I think of all this now, I wish I'd been less emotional," says Alex. "I don't know what I'd change. I just wish it hadn't happened. I wish I hadn't had to go through it. But, even the times when I was out of line and I really lost it, I think that's sort of normal. I don't like the term 'a good divorce,' but Sam and I were as respectful as we could have been.

"When I do my meditation, I've been sending some loving kindness toward Sam and Erika. I want Sam to be happy, and she does make him happy. She's given him what I haven't been able to, and it doesn't make me any less."

Alex puts it well. She does not have to be less. And she can now allow the connections. These adults have found ways to rearrange and make new lives that are rich for themselves and rich as models for their children.

Now there is a fourth player in the mix. Alex has a new committed relationship. This fourth player has opinions and needs about space and connection, just like the needs for space and connection that Erika brought to the family. Alex and Sam are getting much better at handling the choices around when they want time as parents alone and when they want to include their new partners. They traveled together and proudly watched as their oldest son received his graduate degree. Soon they will gather with their partners to share the religious holidays. It all gets clearer and clearer, over time.

SIX NEW AMERICAN FAMILIES

These are the new American families. All of the adults have gained wisdom in making their journey from being former lovers to kin. As I have said so often in this book, the language used to describe separated families is inaccurate. "Broken" is not useful. "Untangling" and "rearranging" are more accurate in describing what happens as parents move through separations and divorces and on into their new lives apart. They are "kin" and have real connections around children and the extended families. Parents who decide to separate need a picture of possibilities to let them see the creativity and kinship possible once the initial stresses and angers and sadness are understood and accepted.

Recognizing kinship and continuing connection comes at different times. Nan and Carl recognized their lifelong connections right from the start. Ken and June did so, as well. Virginia and Dan continued their connection as their children welcomed a new sibling. Their kinship was enhanced as a younger child was born into their extended family. Some parents are freer to recognize kinship only after the legal and financial requirements are over. Mike and Elaine were able to refind their connection as Mike's parents died and brought them back to their childhood history. Lizabeth learned to support kinship around her children even though she was the only one holding that notion and working to hold connections for her children. Alex, Sam, and Erika have learned how to celebrate religious holidays together. They will have more opportunities to sort out connections as their adult children move into committed relationships and the changes that will bring. They will probably plan weddings and welcome grandchildren together.

Getting cordial isn't the goal. It's recognizing these people are your kin for life. "Let's pull together" is what we say in a crisis or a time of change. The units that pull together these days are very surprising.

All of these families will have photos of weddings and baby showers they never would have imagined—a huge family around their children—all kin. They will have to help second-graders figure out who's in the family and to introduce the next generation to all the complexities of being a family. Of starting to name and include all the people who shape you.

And that's what life is all about—the making and remaking of relationships. Finding kin.

8

Stories of Double Pioneers: Lesbian and Gay Families Recognize Kinship

Wisdom for Separated Parents is based on interviews with more than 50 men and women. It is not surprising, therefore, to find that six of the family stories of untangling and rearranging involve questions of sexual orientation.

It is difficult to get accurate data on how much of the population is gay, lesbian, or bisexual, but many gay and lesbian therapists suggest that it is 1 in 10.[1,2] It has been relatively uncommon to include discussions of differing sexual orientations in general parenting books. Today, this is changing. When these six parents were struggling with how to separate and stay respectfully connected, no books were available.

In the gay and lesbian community, it was difficult to find support as a parent. Not until the mid-'80s did Boston have an organization, Gay and Lesbian Counseling Services,[3] offering help and support to gay and lesbian parents.

So the men and women separating in the 1960s who went on to form gay and lesbian partnerships were double pioneers. Here are six stories of those pioneers. They untangled and rearranged from the 1960s to the 1990s. Not only were these parents pioneers in continuing to care for their children and staying connected with their former partner after separation, but also they faced and lived through the enormous cultural changes that brought gender orientation out of the closet—and brought gay parenting out, as well.[4]

AL'S STORY

I always wondered if I loved Susan. But I know now that I did love her because I don't anymore. I realize now that we wouldn't have made it anyway because of the issues that she had. It wasn't because of my homosexuality. We really tried. (married 1957, separated 1967, divorced 1969, interviewed 2006)

Al met his future wife, Susan, in the early 1950s, when they were high school students in a small manufacturing city in upstate New York. Having been born into a family of dancers, he was encouraged to "give it a try" and moved to New York City to push the limits of his talent. Two years of study prepared him to return home to be a part of the family dance business.

As he returned, in the late 1950s, the social, religious and family prompts were to marry, have kids, and "settle down." So he proposed to Susan and married in a Catholic ceremony. He loved adventure and decided to sign up for the army before joining the family business. He took his bride to Alabama for his two years of military service. The couple did find adventure and connection during his stint. They met other couples and played bridge and gave parties and decided to begin a family. "My early marriage was full with social plans and new ways of life. I loved that time in my life." The couple and their two children were embedded in a large and protected social circle. The hustle and bustle of having small children was fun for them, and they were far enough away from their family expectations to develop new patterns of being partners and parents.

"When my hitch was over, we came back to our hometown with two kids and one on the way. We settled into life in the family dance business." Returning home meant returning to strong and troubled family patterns. Both Al and Susan had families with multiple problems through many generations. "We didn't have baggage; we had trunks of troubles in our families." Both were trying to escape long histories of family alcoholism and sexual infidelities. Neither of these issues was easily talked about in the 1950s.[5] In alcoholic families, there are often too many words, or too much angry acting out, or too much unfocused feeling. Hardly ever quiet talking about family problems. And sex in the 1950s was something that you might do—but not talk about.

So it was not surprising when Al and Susan became entwined in the troubling patterns of anger, sexual confusion, betrayal, and alcoholism that were their family legacy. And they were alone with it. They did not know how to talk about all of this—together or with friends. They had no models for how to talk. They accepted that sex and alcoholism were secrets, and became mired in the angry tension without resolution. They felt the public requirements of "perfection" and "togetherness" of the 1950s and "as good Catholics [they] didn't have a clue about how to ask any questions."

Al had experimented with homosexual relationships in high school and when living in New York City. As trouble began to brew in the marriage, he turned to those familiar relationships again. But now he was tortured by his choices. He saw himself as a father and a "good" Catholic and didn't know how to understand his bisexuality. "Sex was always good with Susan, and I really enjoyed it. But all the screaming and hollering about other things was just awful. I grew up with that, and I didn't think it was healthy for the kids."

He began to look for help with his sexual questions. Such help was extremely limited and judgmental, if available at all. Homosexuality was considered a mental illness until 1973, when the American Psychiatric Association removed sexual orientation from its diagnostic list of mental problems.[6] For Al, in 1962, the only option was a month-long program at a local mental hospital that claimed to "cure" homosexual feelings and behaviors. Al wanted to be committed to his wife, sexually and emotionally, and wanted deeply to have his children grow up in a traditional family. He agreed to the month-long hospitalization.

"I was working my butt off to be everything I thought I was supposed to be. I was part-way through a program when she told me she was having an affair. That's when I was hurt because I was really working to save that marriage. I never finished the program.

"We struggled along for a while, and I kept thinking her affair would stop. It never stopped until the guy's marriage was broken up. Then she didn't want him. And, by that time, I didn't want her. I just didn't want to go through the turmoil. I just wanted out.

"The whole town was talking about my being in the hospital, and then our separation came out. I held my head up, and I found out who my friends were. I didn't feel that our friends chose sides. They just dropped both of us."

This family had been oozing apart for a long while. With their divorce, in 1969, they became a statistic. People looking at the public facts of this family would see the "popular" picture of a split, divorced, broken family with single parents. But what is a "broken" family? "I never thought of my family as broken. A little dysfunctional, maybe, but not broken."

As soon as the separation was on the table, both Al and Susan could deal with each other again and could be very practical. They had been good partners on many levels. They just could not cope with the extraordinary tensions of the sexual issues for both of them. Once they were no longer hurting each other as lovers, they were able to figure out how to care for the children and deal with the financial and legal questions.

"We sat down with all the kids. We told them we were getting a divorce and that they were all going to live with Mom. My 10-year-old son was very independent and very creative. He said he'd rather live with his best friend, not Mom. Don't you just love that? I told him he had to live with Mom but that he'd still be able to see his friend.

"I moved out. I could see the kids any time I wanted. I just thought the fighting had to stop. I couldn't stand it." Al was crying as he told his story more than 40 years after the separation.

Al and Susan "worked out all the money issues. We did have a lawyer at the end but mostly worked everything out ourselves. The lawyer didn't want us to do it this way." Remember joint custody wasn't legally available until 1980.[7] "But we were clear what we wanted and how much I could afford to give. I was insistent on no alimony. Child support went on until each kid was

18, but then I contributed to college and all that stuff. We never changed the financial agreement, although I do remember that when the kids were in college she needed a new car, so I paid for that."

After the separation and divorce, Al went on to create a rich and rewarding life for himself and his three children—and stayed connected with Susan.

He had a fairly formal and traditional picture of family. Al wanted that picture for his children and was the driver behind shaping the process of rearranging. When Susan needed to move for work, he followed. They set up their new lives so that he could stay connected with his children.

Al became a caretaker for a large rural property so that the kids could spend every summer with him. He made sure that the kids stayed close to Susan's family and that his own family did not turn their back on Susan. "To this day, Susan visits my mother every time she goes back to town to see her family."

In 1980, years after his divorce, Al met and fell in love with his life partner. Together, they made a family for his children. "Ralph was real good with those kids. We took them on lots of trips. I remember, one Father's Day, he showed up with all three kids. It was the greatest surprise. He arranged it all with Susan.

"Ralph was a father to them. They liked him. They still like him. They used to call him the Teacher of Manners. Now that the grandkids are here, they call him Grumpy."

With all three children now in their 40s, Al has provided a substantial role model for continued family connection. The children and grandchildren stay connected with their mother and their father. They are aware of the gift that Al and Ralph gave them in living a long and loving relationship. When asked whether he can be proud of being such a good model, Al says, "But I had no idea what I was doing. It just sort of happened. I don't feel I was ever in control. Maybe I was, but I certainly didn't feel it."

Al and Ralph moved to the Southwest in retirement and stay in touch with Susan. "We send e-mails to catch up on what the kids and grandkids are doing. When we meet, I give her a kiss and a hug. I still do. I hug everybody now."

But there are issues and difficulties between them. "After Ralph and I retired, we'd have the kids out here, and I would invite Susan, too. She came a few times, but it really didn't work out well. She knows how to push everybody's buttons. So now the kids and grandkids come, but I promised I wouldn't ask Susan if they didn't want her. They usually say, 'We don't want Mom to come.' I suppose if I was back in New York and my daughter was having Christmas, we'd both be there. But, I wouldn't arrange it again." Susan and Al are kin, but she's an annoying member of his kinship circle. And every family has one or two of those.

"I like the connection with Susan when we are alone." They can have long talks and remember shared experiences of their early life together. They can do practical things, but Susan annoys every member of the family. So, like many circles of kin, Al and Susan find ways to share what they can. "We might get to a high school reunion at the same time. I think that'd be a hoot. Can you imagine the reaction? All those old friends who dropped us both!"

On top of the inherited family troubles, it was the torture of bisexuality that put pressure on Al and then on the couple. Susan's infidelity set the stage for the split. They were courageous to separate in 1967 as Catholics and as residents of a small community.

Al's early family life with Susan was happy and connected. He wanted—and had—a traditional life with his children, and he went on to create another conventional family with Ralph. Creating and maintaining the benign space while responding to the need for rearranging was taken on by Al. He stayed close to Susan in order to ensure solid connections for his children. He knew that they would remain kin right from the start. The kids were young enough to have plenty of time to live with their new stepfather and to feel the sense of family provided by Al's new partnership.

TOM'S STORY

> She and her new husband had some financial help from me, but they took care of the household. I stayed out of their finances. I realize that her husband really raised my daughter. He was the father on a daily basis. I have to be respectful of everything he's done. (married 1965, separated 1969, divorced 1969, interviewed 2006)

Gay and lesbian issues grab headlines. The stories here are *not* sensational. They are about ordinary parents sorting out their first marriages, staying devoted to children, and choosing new life partners. In the '60s and '70s, there was no popular way to think of the possibility of a parent with a homosexual identity.[3] Stonewall (1969) had not happened, and Gay Pride had not yet been whispered.[8]

Al was courageous in staying close to the traditional family he had always wanted. Tom had a different sense of family. He had no particular religious heritage and no particular drive after college. He joined the Peace Corps in 1964. During training, he and Patty quickly became pals. They were offered an assignment in a remote South American village, and these pals very much wanted to continue to work together. They were not lovers but were advised to marry in order to find acceptance in their assigned traditional community. Two single American young people living together would not have gathered the respect they needed for their Peace Corps work. During their assignment, they moved easily together "in an isolated cocoon" and found the work extremely rewarding.

After the Peace Corps, they moved easily into the next stage of married life. They chose graduate school in Chicago. Hard work, many friends, and a baby were part of grad student life. But, he reflects, "We had been in two protective environments for our whole marriage, the Peace Corps and the university."

Tom brought to marriage questions of sexual orientation that had been simmering in adolescence but that had not bubbled to the surface in the protective environments of the Peace Corps and early graduate study. Then, in the sexual turmoil of the late '60s, he began to feel permission to take his questions seriously. That was easy to do on a major university campus. "I was just starting to be active in the gay scene, and there was a lot of opportunity and support in the university setting."

A serious medical emergency brought his life and sexual questions into focus. Hospitalized with a life-threatening illness, he found that his fear of death propelled him to disclose his sexual orientation to Patty. Once it was spoken, there was an immediate split. Literally, over a weekend. He had no way of imagining being gay and continuing to father in the conventional ways. And Patty had no way of wrapping her mind around continuing in a situation so out of her expected notions of family.

With the life-threatening illness resolved, they began to move toward divorce. "It was sad at the beginning. We didn't so much as agree that we were going to get the divorce, it just sort of was the unstated truth. She filed for the divorce, and I didn't contest it. It was as close to a do-it-yourself divorce that you can get. Patty went to the legal clinic at the university, and they did it for her. I didn't have a lawyer. I just signed the papers."

Tom moved out of the family home and saw his daughter a couple of times a week while he taught at the university. His notion was that Patty was now the parent.

One of the hardest aspects of the separation for Tom was the moment of telling his fairly stiff and conservative parents. Telling them about the divorce meant telling them he was gay. "That was pretty intense. Mother was more accepting than Father. He was a macho soul. A sad part is that my mother had only limited access to her granddaughter after that. It just wasn't comfortable for anyone. I think she really wanted to be involved with her granddaughter, but she never knew how." Both parents were more upset about sexual issues than about separation and divorce. In this family, the questions of sexual orientation, not the divorce, created family alienation in sad and serious ways.

Within a year of the separation, Tom took a teaching post about five hours away, in Wisconsin. He continued to visit every couple of months. Patty stayed in the original home and remarried fairly quickly. "The original terms were set by the divorce, and I always met all the terms and requirements of the child support. Then I kicked in anything I thought I could afford for special occasions, graduations, or a trip or something like that and a little extra at birthdays and Christmas."

Tom became very much the typical "visiting Dad" rather than a co-parent on a daily basis. "Patty made it very easy when I visited my daughter. She'd plan little events. She'd suggest taking her to the zoo or to an exhibit on Indians." Tom relied very much on Patty to direct the parenting. He was more an uncle.

His academic career took him in many directions over the years. He never lost touch with his daughter or with Patty. But his daughter was parented, on a daily basis, by Patty and her second husband. After many moves, in the United States and abroad, and two other relationships, he is now retired with his long-term partner, living in North Carolina.

The couple connections between Tom and Patty are not as vibrant or as troubled as those between Al and Susan. But Tom and Patty's connection was not broken and is uncomplicated even today. "Now when I'm near Chicago, my partner and I go to dinner with Patty and her husband. They take us out to dinner. When any kind of occasion happens, like my daughter's wedding, my partner and I are always a part of it. I was surprised and pleased to be involved in the wedding. I had thought that because I had opted out so early in her life that I wasn't going to be a part of these major occasions. Patty and her husband included me in the plans for the wedding, but usually after they were pretty set. I gave the bride away. I thought that was quite an honor and very gracious of Patty's husband."

In this family, it was Patty who took the lead in keeping the kinship connection. Tom didn't turn his back but didn't know how or feel he had a right to take the lead in family matters. Grandchildren are now part of the mix, and "my daughter tries very hard to make me a celebrity when we go to see the boys. They visited here, and it was lots of fun." He was not cut off from his grandchildren as his mother had been.

"It's about as good as it can get. It's respectful and warm, but you know there's a certain distance. It's not at all awkward. But it's not exactly a storybook ending. It's all very civilized and more about continuation—something that's not over, just changed."

1980s AND 1990s

Our culture has changed and stretched to include gay and lesbian life as an ordinary sexual orientation, no longer the moral or psychiatric issue it was in the '50s. However, lesbian and gay parents had additional struggles to become visible and find a place. It was still out of the ordinary in the '70s and '80s to be a parent and to be gay or lesbian. These adults were well under the cultural radar in both the straight and gay and lesbian worlds. By the 1990s, the number of openly gay or lesbian parents had grown.

Four family stories come from that time. Although sexual orientation was a factor in the adult decisions in these families, these new family connections were now in a culture of permission. Sexual questions could be openly addressed, if not universally accepted. Rachel's, Emily's, Donna's, and Sheila's stories unfold at a time when schools and community groups, especially those in larger urban areas, were learning to accept gay and lesbian parents with more openness.

RACHEL'S STORY

All of this was pretty amiable. It was our personal dynamic that was very difficult. The upheaval wasn't because of his new relationship or mine. Or even because of being a lesbian. It was his increasing alcoholism or my increasing awareness or both. At first, I didn't know he was an alcoholic. We had a group of friends who drank like him, so I thought it was more or less normal. (married 1978, separated 1985, divorced 1985, interviewed 2007)

Rachel married Evan in Oklahoma. They met at 14 and were dating at 18 and "by junior year in college were engaged." They married the following summer.

"He was a difficult guy right from the start. He was an alcoholic, but I didn't call it that then. All of his troubles felt sort of tolerable to me until I had a baby in our second year of marriage. Then I just didn't have the extra energy to look after him, too. When my daughter was two, I just hit the wall."

She broached the idea of a temporary separation. "We weren't really angry. We weren't really friendly. I was just tired. I just said, 'Can we take a break?' And he went out and got an apartment! I really thought we were just going to take a break. Then he met this other woman, and we never could put it back together. That's probably where we were going anyway." She was the lead in using language to speak of separation, but he seems to have been waiting for the chance to leave. He acted. The question of sexual orientation was not the centerpiece of the trouble.

Rachel had always been a woman to march to her own drummer. She had been interested in women sexually. Taking this window of opportunity, she began a new relationship "right away after the separation—for companionship and sex. For starters, I was Jewish in Oklahoma, and my life was so outside the norm of anybody that I knew, Jewish or not. I was getting divorced with a baby and coming out as a lesbian. My family just kind of ignored it, all of it. His alcoholism, the sexuality. I just didn't really care what they thought."

Rachel and Evan established a nesting arrangement[9] for their toddler. They took turns living in the house. "Our daughter was only two. We went back and forth for one year. That part of it was pretty amiable. Parenting was easy. He deferred. He was very respectful of me as a parent, so that worked for me. He never had a lawyer. I just hired a lawyer and told him how it was going to be, and he signed the papers."

Once these parents had a settlement and the divorce was final, Evan moved back to the family home, and Rachel bought a little house. Rachel was the primary parent, and their growing daughter went to her dad's house every other weekend and on the weekday evenings when Rachel taught at university.

Evan's new marriage and new child did not disrupt the established plans. Parenting decisions went smoothly, primarily because Evan let Rachel take the lead and Evan's new partner accepted this arrangement.

These two parents always had adequate and independent financial resources. "He didn't ever pay me child support. He was supposed to, and occasionally he would send a check for $10,000. He would always say he was going to pay regularly, but he never did. He wasn't trying to deny me the money. He's just not responsible. Evan just couldn't get it together to write a check every month. And I didn't always want to be talking to him about money. I never did anything about it. I was fine financially. Maybe it all equaled out.

"Then I met a woman who became a serious partner. We decided to move to Massachusetts. He wasn't happy about the move. His drinking was escalating, so we had a hard time talking to each other. But he really liked my partner and respected her a lot. She would talk to him and negotiate instead of me."

The move was a big wrench for her daughter and for Evan and the extended family. Rachel's daughter, the first grandchild for both families, was an important person. And now the grandparents would be separated from their granddaughter by many miles. "Everyone was friendly, but it wasn't the same.

"I was relieved when I came to Northampton [Massachusetts]. Everything was easier here. The pressure to conform was much greater in Oklahoma. I had always felt different there.

"After the move, my daughter saw her father about six times a year. He'd fly up here and get her and take her back. So they always had a relationship, and she always saw her grandparents. But I was oblivious to safety with regards to his drinking. When Evan and his new wife came for my daughter's seventh birthday party, they stayed at my house, with my partner and me. He got pretty drunk at the party, and I realized I couldn't trust him to take good care of our daughter on her visits with him. I told him he could come to Massachusetts any time and visit, but, until he had the drinking under control, she couldn't go to Oklahoma. He just accepted that. There were no legal problems in my decision."

At any particular juncture or life change for her daughter, Rachel made the plans and Evan did his part. He and his new wife had a baby. The closeness of her daughter and the new baby happened because Rachel took the lead in fostering the relationship between the half-sibs.

"He and I had a friendly relationship after some years of stress. Then he had a psychotic break two years ago and has withdrawn from everybody. It makes me really sad that he's so sick. I worry about his health. I feel helpless. He won't let anybody near him, not even our daughter."

She worries about how to help her daughter deal with her father's psychotic break and whatever else the future brings. "My daughter has always been very guarded and protective of him. I don't have a lot of information. She has the information. I know she really worries about him a lot." But the two have not found a safe and comfortable way to talk about all of this.

Rachel feels deep sadness for her daughter. "He promised her a big wedding. It's complicated to talk about that with her, because I don't want her to be mad at me or worried. I know he wants to do what he says. But I don't know how to talk of the possibility that he wouldn't be able to come up with the money or be healthy enough to walk her down the aisle or even be at a wedding." Rachel knows, from experience, just how unpredictable Evan is. And, if things go awry, it will be Rachael who picks up the pieces again. And stands by her daughter as she watches her father slip away.

"Prior to the breakdown, he would call me occasionally. Or I would call him, and we would talk. I mean, we had real affection for each other. We'd just check in with each other. We sort of had a nice friendly relationship. There was nothing left to fight about anymore.

"I feel very proud that Evan and I never used our daughter against each other despite all of the mutual dysfunctional stuff. I know it's had an impact on her, but we never really fought over her or used her to hurt each other.

"And I miss him. I miss not being in touch with him. There's all this nostalgia and good feeling now—not trying to erase bad experiences but kind of surprised about the good feelings. Thirty years is a long time. We had a childhood together."

The sadness of this woman's feelings about her former partner is powerful. She has lost a childhood pal as well as the man who is father to her child. She lost him not to separation and divorce but to mental illness. She now carries all the tenderness of that loss and is unable to express it either to him or to her daughter.

EMILY'S STORY

The children are working out an understanding of the kinship relationships. The girls are trying to figure out this great man in their life. My oldest daughter thought he was her ex-Dad because he was my ex-husband. He's not quite a Dad but more than a friend. And he's their guardian. They came up with a name for him: Stad = Stu and Dad. (married 1979, separated 1987, divorced 1987, interviewed 2007)

Emily and Stu were the ideal young Jewish couple. Children of doctors, they married in 1979. "I was the oldest daughter, and he was the ideal husband. The perfect match." They moved to New Haven, Connecticut, and settled down to have the requisite two children, lovely little boys.

"A tragic family death [her brother's] brought everything crashing down around us in 1986." Emily began therapy to grieve. Stu began an affair with one of her friends. They quickly knew they would separate. No fighting. Just sadness and despair.

It was not unusual for me to hear of a major loss preceding a separation. Chronic or sudden illnesses, the death of a child or parents, or major financial losses might set the stage for unbearable tensions in the couple relationship.

Often, the interviewee would see the connection for the first time, or in a new way, as we talked about the long arc of family history. Some knew that the loss would impact their relationship but were so absorbed in daily life that there was little emotional energy available or knowledge about how to manage the impact of the loss. The partners just couldn't grieve together as a couple.

Emily and Stu were just such a couple. For Emily, the experience of a sibling's death brought her face to face with how little time we really have in life. She needed to explore her loss and deeply felt sexual questions. Emily and Stu went into couples therapy but couldn't prevent the slide away from each other into newer, more bearable attachments. As Stu proceeded with his new relationship, Emily became more deeply involved in her individual therapy.

They were able to keep the adult issues of hurt and abandonment separate and to focus on the needs of their small children. "The boys were very little, and we didn't want them to leave their house, so we moved in and out. There was a night-by-night change. He got a place to live part-time, and I stayed with friends. We thought we could both stay in this arrangement for a long while, but he had this new relationship with my old friend, and I just couldn't cope after a few months."

The fact that Stu's new partner had been Emily's close friend was just too much of a strain and too painful an injury for her to endure daily contact. They could not bear the strain of continuing to share space around the boys. "He bought a house quite close. I went and helped decorate and set up the house. We split up the furniture. I made him pillows for the couch. Wasn't that absurd? While he was sleeping with my old friend!

"The kids were the focus. It was really about them. We needed to get over whatever were our issues. I was angry at him. He was angry at me. But I wouldn't tolerate his calling me and hanging up the phone when he was angry. He got the message and got over that. It just took a while.

"We did all the parent conferences together. We went to all the school concerts, too. But not the holidays in the beginning. I just couldn't do that and include my former friend." The parents connected in a civil way, but not with a great deal of warmth.

Emily had dated a few women right from the beginning. "I was really careful when I dated, going out when the kids were at their Dad's. I didn't want them to have to go through lots of changes. They didn't need to be a part of that. There were four or five years that I felt like a single parent. It didn't have to do with Stu not helping and being there for the kids, but there wasn't anyone serious in my life until 1992. I felt single, but I wasn't parenting alone."*

---

*There is an important distinction between being single and being a single parent. The common notion about single parents is that they are all alone in their parenting. Most people who show up in the census as single parents are separated but have a working relationship with their former partner as part of a parenting team.

After several years and some short-term relationships, Emily was able to be more open to the kinship connection with Stu and his wife, her former friend. As she found and settled into "a relationship that could become as rich and as full as the relationship I had had with Stu and the boys," things became more cordial between Stu and Emily.

The relationship deepened between Emily and her new partner, Sharon. They decided to adopt because they wanted children together. "When I was first pregnant with my oldest son and realized it was a boy, I thought, 'Oh, my God, what do I know about raising boys?' The amazing thing is that my baby boy taught me everything I needed to know. So, when Sharon and I decided to adopt, I wanted girls. I really wanted to know about daughters and adoption.

"We adopted two girls who were born in China. Each time we came home with a baby, Stu would be at the airport to greet us with the older boys. He is incredibly generous with the girls, with his time and his money. He says he's never seen two such happy children. The only place they spend an overnight without their moms is with Stu and his wife.

"It wasn't always easy. It was painful in the beginning. Stu and Sharon had to tough it out. Stu used to come into our old house and rummage around in the kitchen and use the house as if it was still his. That just didn't fly with Sharon. One day she made it quite clear that he couldn't do that anymore. It was a boundary thing. He just hadn't realized it wasn't his house anymore.

"I had to come to a different place with his wife, my friend. We had been in a women's group and a mothers' group together. The other women in the groups were just horrified when I started to renew the relationship with her. I had to calm them down and say that this was going to happen because of the boys." Emily was now able to stand up for the kinship connection.

Ultimately, this family created a caring four-parent model for all their children. Emily and Stu and both new partners seem to share equally in the care and concern for all of them. "When my older son graduated from college, we all drove to Pittsburgh together. We rented a van. Stu drove. I was in the van with my partner. His wife was with us and my younger son and the two girls. We even all stayed at the same motel." Seeing this group in a restaurant or as they proudly watched their son graduate wouldn't begin to tell the history of these adults and these children.

"Every time there is a passage and these kids seem to make it to the other side, Stu and I connect. There's great tenderness around our parenting. And, on Father's Day, there's nobody else I could have imagined raising my sons with. He's a remarkable father. He just happens to be a man. It wasn't in the cards for me."

DONNA'S STORY

I think our positive relationship has been more possible because his partner is a man. It would have been very different had it been a woman.

The fact that Brad was gay relieved the shame of having failed at marriage. That has helped me. If we divorced, I don't think he would marry again, even though it's going to be legal soon. I think he feels some sort of responsibility to me and finds it comforting that there's some kind of attachment out there in the world. He seems to take pleasure in the fact that we're still married. When he introduces me, he says, "This is my wife." That's infuriating. (married 1973, separated 1995, not yet divorced, interviewed 2008)

"We're still not officially divorced," says Donna with a chuckle. "We'll never be in the divorce statistics. But we've been separated since 1995. It will probably be pending forever.

"We met in San Francisco when Brad was in the navy. I was 28. We had two years of courting, but it was spotty. We never spent a lot of time together. I don't think you would call it dating. I was just kind of there to entertain him." They drifted along together, and she followed when he went to law school in New York. When she got to the other side of the country, she was horrified to think of how her very WASP family and their friends would react to a couple alone in a distant city. "I told him if we move in together, you have to give me a ring—and Brad got that ring! He found me an apartment, and he had an apartment. The apartments were back to back. We ended up putting all our furniture in one and living in the other. All the little old ladies in his family thought it was swell that we were living separately."

Familiar life patterns pushed them along. Both worked, and, when the children came along, they moved out of the city and into the suburbs in Connecticut. "We had two boys and were living a fairly traditional upper-middle-class life in the suburbs. I found out he was gay four years before we separated. I found out by accident when I looked in his briefcase. I was looking for a map, and I found a love letter from a man. I had to read it about 10 times as it sunk in.

"His mother had died that year, and, as I piece it together now, as soon as both parents were gone, he started exploring his sexual orientation. Brad traveled a lot and had started going to gay bars.

"When I found that letter, we were in the middle of designing a new house. He was completely compartmentalizing what he was doing. All the while, he was going to gay bars and to gay father's meetings[10] and still pursuing our relationship and allowing me to get wrapped up in building this house. When I confronted him with the letter, he said he had no intention about leaving the marriage.

"It was awful. He saw himself as bisexual, so it wasn't a conflict for him. We went to couples therapy. He said he wanted to work on our relationship. He wanted to see if our relationship could meet his needs. But our sex life was pretty dead by then. I didn't want to work on that part of our relationship if it was going to just blow up.

"He was totally confused and totally acting out. That was so surprising because he is such a straight arrow, boringly so. For four years, we struggled in therapy before we told the kids that we were separating.

"We spent a lot of time trying to figure out how to tell the kids. There were lots of questions. Do you tell them that your dad is gay? Do you tell them that we're separating and that your dad is gay at the same time? Do you say we're separating and not tell them why? We were very emotionally distant, and the boys felt that. They knew at some level that something was wrong. They were 12 and 16. We finally told them during the summer on a Long Island beach. As soon as we said the word 'separation,' our older son just took off like a blast. He used every four-letter word that he could think of. The younger one just disappeared into his hat and started to cry. Those moments are so etched. To be hurting your kids like that.

"I asked Brad to go to Los Angeles to tell my parents. They hadn't been east to visit since our youngest was 18 months old. I wanted him to tell them he was gay and that was why we were separating. Telling my southern California conservative Republican parents? I couldn't do it. I always felt criticized by my parents. They always wanted to see me with a life that went just right. After he told them, my parents didn't call me for five weeks.

"And today he and I are financially all tied up. We've shared his income since we separated. Now that he's going into retirement, that will be changing. We've been doing this all through a financial adviser for the last 13 years. We had no mediators or lawyers.

"Just the other day, a lot of emotions came up for me. Our son is to be married, and his fiancée wanted to see my wedding dress. I went to the closet. I hadn't seen the dress since our marriage, 30 years ago. I opened it up and started to cry. It's just so sad. That afternoon we went to a meeting with the financial adviser. So there I was with two men, trying to talk about finances and feeling so upset. I said, 'I pulled out my wedding dress this morning and exploded into tears again. I don't think they had a clue as to the sad meaning of that dress.

"We left that meeting, and we had the most honest conversation that we ever had. I said to Brad, 'You ended up with the life you wanted and what I wanted in life was just destroyed. I still want that intact family.'

"I share holidays with him now. At first I wouldn't. I was too hurt. But now he comes for Christmas Day. What I wanted from life was a family and community that I didn't have growing up. That's what I was trying to create. That was my number one priority. The longing for that never really left. So gradually I began to bring him back for the family gatherings. Thanksgiving was sort of off limits for a time, and he seems to have weaseled back into that. His new partner is always part of all the holidays, too.

"Mostly we keep our distance. But this Christmas, for some reason, I hugged him. It felt like kind of dangerous territory. I think there's also some level of attachment there for me. I could imagine being married to a gay man and going through all this and being close. I could imagine that, but Brad is so limited emotionally. Whether he's gay or not, he just can't do that intimacy part. I sometimes get into a lot of pain around missing the companionship and missing all the good things that would have happened had I stayed with him. But emotionally it would have been empty. I have to remember that."

Donna doesn't yet know what is best for her in this complicated family history. The upcoming wedding of her son may help to clarify her next steps. These life events are often the opportunity for shifts in relationships and clarity about future options.

"We shared the dog until recently. When we first separated, he suggested giving the dog away. I couldn't believe that he could be so emotionally detached that he could give away the dog. It's no wonder he can walk away from this marriage without sadness. The kids would never have forgiven us if we'd given up that dog. So Brad took the dog on weekends, just like visiting with the kids. He'd come all the way out from the city and back again, even after the kids had gone to college.

"Just a few months ago, the dog got quite sick and we had to put him down. I knew I couldn't be alone that last night. Brad came out and stayed overnight. We did it all together, holding the dog until he died. Afterward, I just collapsed in Brad's arms. He held me, and we both wept. And that felt wonderful and strange. I got an e-mail from Brad the other day, saying that he missed me. He was thinking of all the casual connections that we'd had when we passed the dog back and forth every other weekend. He said it was so sad that it had ended. This, from a guy who is not usually very demonstrative or affectionate!"

SHEILA'S STORY

We realized what would work for us. We really did want to work together to co-parent our children. We love them. His involvement with gay fathering and mine with the Straight Spouse Network[11] really helped shape how we parented. I truly did not feel all alone. There were all these other people going though the same things. You don't feel so ashamed. Being gay isn't as hard as what a lot of people put up with— like alcoholism and abuse. That's what attracted me to Chris. He didn't drink and he was social and he wanted to have fun. Life wasn't a big tragedy. He danced and sang. (married 1983, separated 1997, divorced 2003, interviewed 2009)

"We had totally different backgrounds. He's Greek. I'm Irish and French. One thing I know about myself is I have a comfortable curiosity about life. I don't have a fear of change. I was never interested to marry someone from my neighborhood. I felt like marrying someone with my same background was just going to be a life sentence.

"I knew of his sexuality when I married him. We never really discussed it. We had a good time together. We just really enjoyed each other. We moved to California and weren't around our families. We were just together, and we had to depend on one another. Sexuality between us wasn't an issue. I felt like we had a very good sex life together. We absolutely were interested in one another, and it was pretty healthy.

"Things shifted about three years into our marriage. I had a job as a sales rep, and I traveled all the time. I came home one time after two weeks, and I went to the doctor. I had had a miscarriage, and the doctor discovered that I had herpes. When I told Chris, he didn't say anything. And then, in the middle of that night, he couldn't sleep. He told me he had gone to a bookstore and that he was having sex with men. At that point, I wanted to leave. He begged me to stay and said it was never going to happen again. So I sort of believed him.

"After the herpes, I don't want to say I didn't trust him, but I would argue with him about things. What I was really arguing about was that he was gay. It never really came out in the arguments. A couple of times we came very close to addressing it. I guess we decided we had two little kids, so why go there? It was hard.

"We moved back to our hometown in Rhode Island. Our kids were four and two, and we knew we could get some help from our parents. I was the main worker, and I needed the support of my family and my parents. His parents were close and were really good support, too.

"Chris was working as a waiter at night. That's when it all started to fall apart. He was out with gay friends who were also waiters. They went out to bars and stuff, and it just started unraveling."

At that point, Chris and Sheila decided to separate. "I really wasn't telling many people that he was gay. I told some really close friends, but not even my family right away. I would just say that we're separating, that he didn't want to be married.

"He was going to leave at Thanksgiving. Then, in November, my mother had a stroke, so he stayed into the new year. He slept in the basement. We talked a lot at night about what was going on for us and with my mother. He was very, very fond of my mother. He got an apartment and moved out in March. My mother died in April. I had a lot of loss at that time.

"We went to see a family therapist to see how we were going to help tell the kids. It was helpful, but I was angry with both the couples therapist and the family therapist, because I thought that they really sided with Chris. It was more about how he was going to be authentic, more about Chris coming out and being comfortable with himself, and it wasn't much about how I was going to deal with it. I was able to communicate that to both therapists. They both denied that that's the way they were treating us, but I said, 'Well, that's the way I'm feeling.' Later, the couples therapist apologized. The other one didn't.

"We told the children together. We sat in this living room where I'm sitting now. They both cried. It was very sad. I knew the real reason why he left, so it was confusing.

"I stayed in the house, and he gave me a certain amount of money. I had a full-time job. We never had a lawyer until we divorced, six years later. He just said what he was going to pay, and I did everything else. He was always responsible. I always had the health insurance with my job.

"Telling the kids about the separation was separate from telling about the sexuality. We knew that we were going to tell them, but not at the time we separated. We never discussed the sexuality until a year after he left. They were 7 and 10. He was very much involved in the gay dad's group. The crisis time was when he called and said he wanted to take the kids to the circus with the gay fathers' group. I told him no, but my heart was in my feet. I was afraid, and I didn't know what was right. I didn't want to feel this way again, so I went to a straight-spouse support group and said I need help with this. That was the place I needed to be. Everyone was very supportive.

"We ended up telling them about the sexuality individually. When I talked about it, I would say this: 'Well, that's just one part of your father. Think of it as a piece of a pie. That's just a little piece of who he is. The rest is the same.'

"I did that with the divorce, too. They never knew we were divorced until about a month after we got the legal divorce. I told them in the car. I used to tell them things in the car, because kids are captive there. They have to listen. I was driving home and said, 'I forgot to tell you I got divorced.' They said, 'Why didn't you tell us?' And I said, 'Well, because things haven't changed. There's no difference. It's just legal.' I thought it all out. I remember when I brought the second baby home, my mother told me I should just treat the baby like she's been there forever. Don't make a big deal of the change.

"From early on, I never treated Chris gingerly. I never set up play dates and stuff. He always took the kids to school things and to their friend's houses. He would call the other parents to make arrangements, not me. He was very capable and had a flexible schedule. I was working and traveling a lot. We both had to do things to make it work. I didn't make it easier for him. They were his children, too."

They were divorced six years after the separation. "Legally, we needed to do it because he was buying a house." Both were very close and supportive during all those years. "When I had surgery, he took me and signed me in. I had a radical hysterectomy with cervical cancer. He took care of me. He had no issue with any of the physical care. And, yet, there are times of impatience. He could be really nasty, and I could be nasty to him and that's just normal. Mostly, I try to treat him with respect.

"My philosophy of parenting is that we are a safety net. Our kids can bounce and bounce and bounce around in the net. It's our job to make sure they don't fall through and, when they do fall through, to push them back up. They have to learn why they fell through the net, and we have to help them to learn why they fell through. I think I'm much more confident in my parenting after all this with Chris. I'm much more honest and can do a lot of tough love and say things that aren't comfortable to say. It's the kind of parenting I did not have. I use much more language with my children."

Their connection as parents was tested this year with news of their daughter's pregnancy. There were struggles for Chris and for Sheila as they watched their very young daughter make the tough choice to have her baby. They each had moments of thinking about abortion. The parents kept talking, and sometimes yelling, with each other and with their daughter as they all reacted with strong mixed feelings around the pregnancy. "We have a bond. We don't finish the sentence for one another, but we have complete conversations. He understands what I'm saying, and I understand what he's saying. I've always had that with him. We balanced each other out. Angry, sad, everything. So we were able to help our daughter."

The baby was born, and, because of the conflict and the talk, the parents and grandparents were ready to welcome this new family member. Both parents were at the hospital waiting with their son and the baby's father. After spending time with the new mother and the baby, they all went out to dinner—their son, the baby's father, Chris's life partner, and Sheila. At dinner, Sheila felt warm and close, especially to Chris's partner. She thanked him for being gracious and loving to her children. The baby delivered a new level of recognition of kinship.

The day following the birth, Chris's sister invited a large group of family members to welcome the new baby. Sheila had not felt included in his family for quite some time. "My family's always been very nice to him. He still thinks of himself as part of my family. But there's lots of struggle in his family, and I was excluded for a long time. When we went to his sister's house, I hadn't seen these people in years. The next day, I called his sister and said, 'We've had a complex relationship over the years, but I missed you.' She asked me if I was comfortable being with the family again. I said, 'Well, Chris and I are comfortable.' So I guess they'll get used to us being together again. I've come a long way.

"I feel so badly for people who are divorced and are so bitter and can't connect. Those are the times that give you so much hope and faith in life. When you need someone and you can call on them and you just know they're going to be there. Isn't that what life's all about?"

REARRANGING

And that is very true. Separated parents want to be able to count on each other, and these six couples have found creative ways to do just that.

In each of these stories, the original couples stretched to include new notions of parenting in same-sex partnerships. Sometimes, the extended family could stretch, as well. Al's mother accepted the new family. Tom's mother did not, making it impossible for her to continue to be a part of her granddaughter's life. The connection between Sheila's family and Chris's brothers was strong right from the beginning. On the other hand, Chris's siblings only recently came to include Sheila after the birth of the new baby. Rachel's parents were far away and quite passive. Donna knew her very conventional parents would be unable to stretch.

For Al and Tom, the timing of their questions about sexuality was crucial. The early 1950s to the late 1960s was an opening time. Al had to face the burden of being seen as mentally defective. His separation fit more the constriction of the early '50s, the narrowness of the culture, and the concepts of mental health. The family history of sexual acting out and the legacy of alcoholic anger in the family made things messier between Al and Susan.

It was far simpler for Tom. Being openly gay was not as shocking in a university setting in 1969. His mental health was not questioned as Al's had been. What Tom and his wife had to face was a stumbling block of not being able to imagine being gay and co-parenting. They had no models in either the straight or the gay community at that time.

Tom's clear choice of a gay lifestyle, giving permission to his wife and new partner to be the primary parents, made life simpler. Joint custody was not in the law books until 1980,[7] so he did not have that option, nor did he seem to have the internal push to keep the connections as a day-to-day father. That seemed to be a part of his family's style. His mother didn't push to see her granddaughter. He became more a deeply loved uncle, not a full co-parent.

Al had much deeper yearnings for a "traditional lifestyle." He managed to be in a "traditional" marriage with Susan and then to re-create a "traditional" two-parent family with Ralph for more than 30 years.

Al, Tom, and Rachel had marriages that oozed apart. Emily's and Sheila's separations were more sudden. Emily finally saw the alcoholism. Sheila, having come to terms with Chris's early sexual revelations, reacted to the renewed exploration of gay sex and then found it necessary to separate. Donna and her husband are in the stuck-like-Velcro category. They have ties that are both loose and very strong. They seem very capable of bearing the mix of the many levels of attachment for right now.

In three of these families, one parent made the crucial decisions. Evan deferred to Rachel, and Tom deferred to Patty. They were not co-parents. Al took the lead in staying connected and was a full co-parent. Sheila and Chris had established a solid co-parenting system well before any separation was considered. Emily and Stu have the clearest story of joint custody presented here, ultimately expanding it to a four-parent connection that really works for them.

Today, five of the families continue to have connections. Rachel's angst about her former husband's mental illness is a tragedy for her. It also creates a deep divide with her daughter. It is heartbreaking to hear her sadness and to wonder how she will ever be able to let her daughter know how deeply she cared for the man who is slipping away from both of them.

Donna worries about how her boys are managing. "I wonder about the boys a lot. Right after the separation, as our youngest entered high school, he went to Europe for a special program. On his trip, he didn't tell a soul about his father and the separation. The next year, he spent a whole summer with a girl whose mother is lesbian, but he didn't talk to her about it, either. In school, there was no support for kids with gay parents. There is support and celebration for gay kids as they disclose their sexual orientation. But what about kids with gay parents?"[12] How do we help the kids find language to talk about this and to find stories that affirm the normalness of their parents' struggles? We need to let them know that many families move into the future with parents like the ones in these stories—connected and cordial.

These parents will continue to come to terms with changes in the straight and gay communities and the understanding of family and of family separation in the larger society. Just this year, in my private practice, I have been consulted by couples who are separating in order to establish new same-sex partnerships and by couples who have lived for many years in committed partnerships but who are now considering exploring bisexual relationships. Parents can talk about these shifts more easily than they could 40 years ago. However, the pain and sadness and loss are the same. And the process of moving from former lovers to co-parents, the process of untangling and rearranging, still takes time. And it takes a lot of work to create the space for the benign energy to grow.

Becoming Partners Again?

We all fantasize about spinning the world backward, to youth and energy and roads not taken. Maybe all separated parents, on any given day, have their own thoughts about spinning backward, about putting things back together again. The exceptions, most often, are people fleeing from abuse. But not always.

> I was afraid of him. After we separated, he remarried, a very short marriage. I actually spent some time with him after that relationship ended. We did some things with my son. It was a very short period of time, but I just couldn't seem to get away from the drama with him.

This reconnection was a blip in the long process of popping apart the powerful attachment in a stuck-like-Velcro relationship. Even with all the troubles, she agreed to date him again.

FANTASIES

Other parents have serious yearnings over time, serious regrets at other times. There are lots of ways to struggle with "what ifs." Here's a couple who met in Europe.

> We came to the United States and married in 1979. At that time, there were not that many interracial couples around. It was very important to make it work. I think that we were in battle mode against the culture.[1] That helped us to rally together and overlook some things about our relationship. It was us against the world. I might have questioned a lot of things much earlier if we hadn't had to face the racial questions in such a united way.
> After we divorced I had several relationships, and when those relationships ended, I always regretted having split up. I always wondered

if there was another chance with him. I never, ever expressed that to him. But internally that's where I went with my thoughts. I think he was hoping that, too, but he never said anything either. I wonder, if he had said something or if I'd seen an effort on his part, whether we could have gotten back together. But I think there was just too much pride. Now it's very clear there's no chance in the world, because we are just so far apart. (married 1979, separated 1991, divorced 1994, interviewed 2008)

When she wonders about reversing decisions, is it partly about returning to that troubled, yet powerfully connected time?

CLARITY IN THERAPY

Trying again in the early years of separation is often temporary. In this case, a short reconciliation gave Kathleen and Sam the time and the tools to separate respectfully and to understand how to go forward. The couple had oozed apart for many years without much talk. Then, suddenly in a moment of anger, they said the words.

In a pretty tumultuous way, with a lot of arguing one night, we decided to separate. The next day Sam called crying and apologized. So we decided to try again. That stubborn part of me said, "I'm going to make this work no matter what!"

We went to therapy, and we were doing quite well actually and coming together in less angry ways. He was staying home much more. I would say the quality of our life on a day-to-day basis was improving. Sam was a fun father for the kids, very silly and playful with them. But I think, at the bottom of it, we both knew that was temporary. We both needed to change.

The work in therapy did help this couple clear their heads. Kathleen came to understand that she did want the separation.

We moved from being sort of hostile and silent with each other to working together to figure out how to make a separation happen. I just wanted out. I think he came to understand that. But he also needed to know that I was committed to him. When Sam moved several blocks away, I went over and helped him put his place together. I think he did have a sense that I was going to be there for him. He understood that I was going to help him organize around the kids. I was doing the "wifely" function. And I can't say that I did it without resentment and rolling my eyes and being annoyed. But, I felt like I was committed to doing it for the kids. (married 1970, separated 1978, divorced 1981, interviewed 2007)

Therapy helped contain the anger and move through the fear, through the mixed feelings about being together or being apart. Each parent was able to gain some insight into ways to be more predictable and open to each other, to renew trust, and to move into the space of more benign energy. They became partners again and worked well at understanding how to be apart.

A TRIP TOGETHER

Laura actually had a brief experience of being together again, many years after a formal separation and deep into new adult relationships for both partners.

> He and I went together to Israel when our first grandchild was born. It was a long trip, so we had lots of time together. We shared an apartment to cut costs. Our son found an apartment for rent and said, "I know you and dad are going to be sharing an apartment." And then, with some trepidation, he asked, "Are you going to sleep in the same bed?" I gasped, "No, that's why we want two bedrooms." We did have a wonderful time being together as grandparents. As we landed back home, he said, "You know you've been a wonderful traveling companion." That was nice to hear. What I learned after that trip was that I have no fantasy about getting together. *Never!* The thought of living with him is unthinkable. Our styles are so different. Israel was okay. It wasn't permanent, so his habits could be tolerated. Neither of our current partners had a problem with it, so it was a big moment in all our lives. (married 1968, separated 1980, divorced 1981, interviewed 2008)

A REMARRIAGE

Bernadette and Jim actually remarried 19 years after their first separation. They were high school sweethearts and married right after graduation. Kids came along quickly. She stayed home, and he worked two jobs. Jim explains.

> We decided to separate in 1990. Well, she decided more than I. She had been home with kids so long. I was working two jobs to make ends meet. We lost contact—a long, slow process. We both seemed to not be each other's best friend anymore, just drifting apart. We had been married for 25 years. How about this? The day I was in court to get our divorce would have been our 25th wedding anniversary.

After that day in court, they had little contact except for family weddings or christenings. Several years later, he was diagnosed with a kidney disease. His now-grown kids initiated a search for a kidney donor. The children were tested. They asked Bernadette if she would be tested, too. All were potential donors. The family was dealing with hereditary kidney disease, so the kids were advised to save their kidneys in case either was ever diagnosed with the disease. It was a time of deep sadness and anxiety for everyone. Bernadette began to have more contact with Jim and was saddened by the seriousness of the medical condition.

> When I saw him on dialysis, I was really moved. There were no other grandfathers in the family. This man worked so hard, and I wanted him to enjoy the grandchildren. I said to myself, this man's going to be healthy. I'm going to give him a kidney, and that's that. I just wanted him to be a grandfather for a lot longer.

So two surgeries were scheduled and successfully completed. The hospital put Jim and Bernadette in the same room to recover. After discharge from the hospital, they were together a bit longer. Jim again:

> We went to our daughter's house to recuperate. She had just had a baby and had plenty of room. I had the bedroom downstairs, Bernadette had the bedroom upstairs. So we'd see each other at breakfast mostly and during the day. We weren't there too long—maybe a month at most.
>
> Because she had been preparing to be the donor, she had been out of work for three months. I felt so grateful, I started to pay her rent. Then I convinced her to move in for convenience and to save money. It was difficult when we started to live together again. We both had feelings for each other, through the kids and grandchildren. But there were still lots of the old issues there. It was purely platonic for a couple of years. Almost like getting to know each other again. We noticed that we'd grown up a lot.

Bernadette remembers:

> When we came back together, it was more as friends. We were never friends when we were younger. We were husband and wife. He did his thing, and I did mine. All those roles we learned.

Several years passed as these high school sweethearts got to know each other again. Jim remembers:

> We got closer and closer and talked and talked and talked. Not all the time. She had gone back to work. We were still on different shifts, so we were not together a lot. It wasn't like we were sleeping together. It wasn't close like that. We just had to grow on each other again. And then we started to be intimate. Bernadette mentioned getting remarried

once, but I kept putting it off and putting it off. I wanted to make sure that everything was going to work out, and we wouldn't divorce again. Then one day she told me, "I never thought I'd ever fall in love again and have the same feelings I had as a young girl."

Jim weeps as he recounts that moment. Bernadette knows the power of those words, too: "I just love being in love with him. When I say that to him, he just can't even speak."

Bernadette and Jim were originally married in 1965, separated in 1990, and divorced in 1992. They remarried in 2009 in the presence of their children and grandchildren, plus a local reporter who had gotten wind of the story.[2] Local papers had chronicled the earlier headline—"Former Wife Is Kidney Donor"—and wanted to continue a good story.

These kinds of stories will always get the attention of the public and the press. They are interesting and dramatic. It is harder to make a headline out of the slow and steady devotion of two parents apart, the stories that are the centerpieces of this book.

HOW TO KEEP FAMILY, SEPARATELY

One stuck-like-Velcro couple tried again. Linda and Doug met when she was 24. They married, and three children came along soon. Socializing suited both partners. He worked hard and played hard. A busy social life formed a family that looked very connected to the outside world, but there was little intimate connection in the marriage. Linda recalls:

We had an active social life but not an intimate, personal life. I never talked about what it was like. I put up a good front. But, I was hitting the wall with the alcohol.

The moment of clarity and decision came when the family was on a skiing vacation:

He said he'd spend the last day with me, and he got drunk the night before. He was a wreck. I felt terrible and abandoned. He couldn't even get the money for the train trip to the airport. I had no money for me and the three kids. That was the moment. I made excuses for him all these years, and he couldn't do this one thing. I just snapped. I wanted out. I cried the whole way home. When we got home, Doug asked for a formal dinner. I made the dinner. When all the children were seated around the table, he said, "Your mother has asked me for a divorce, and I don't want a divorce. I'm going to have to leave this house." The kids were crying. We all were crying. There was no dinner. He left. I had to handle everything alone, again.

Typical of stuck-like-Velcro parents, the moments of separation are dramatic and may not bring much clarity for anyone—adults or children. These parents had few tools to handle the ambiguity and complexity of their family life.

Struggles about money, mostly hidden money, were constant. When he stopped paying family bills, a trial date was set. The trial brought financial closure, but, true to the deep and abiding connections in these stuck-like-Velcro situations, the following scene was touching and predictive of many moments ahead of them.

Before the trial I noticed Doug sobbing in the hall. I gave him a hug, and I started sobbing. When I had to go before the judge, I was still sobbing. I went home and I cried for three days, because there was just so much emotion that hadn't been expressed.

So, in 1990, Doug and Linda were finally in separate houses and had separated their finances. The community could see them as separated parents, finally divorced. Does this seem like a likely end of story, a good resolution? Not with this couple.

Doug went on to a new love relationship and so did Linda, but they continued to live in the same town and continued to meet in overlapping social circles. They really liked each other. The problems were in their intimate connections—fears that both had about the intensity of sexual and other intimacies when being partners and parents together.

Each of their new relationships went sour at about the same time. Doug called Linda, who worked in real estate, looking for a new apartment. They began spending more time together, and it was clear they both had wishes to try again.

We had a wonderful summer and fall together. There was something deeper about our connection. I think it was because of my experience being in another relationship. I got my old identity back. I had found out what a real relationship could be and was ready to have that with Doug.

Their now-adult children were thrilled, as were their friends.

We planned a big Christmas party for 200 friends. On the eve of that party, he announced that he was leaving again. He said, "I love you but I'm not in love with you, and it is not negotiable."

Now, I am very angry. The other phase I was sad because of what we never had. Now, I'm angry because we had had these months of connection. It was a disaster to tell the kids again. They knew I was devastated. That was the real divorce. That was the worst time of my life. I cried a lot. I couldn't go out of the house. I couldn't stop crying.

Finally, I went to a spiritual counselor. He said I should get back in touch with who I was before I met Doug. I went to a group every Saturday morning. It was very cathartic to see what was playing out in other people's lives. I finally realized that being angry was really negative for me. I didn't like the way I felt. I wanted to kill him. I wanted to hurt him. And that was hurting me. I started letting the anger empower me, not take me down.

And this was the point at which this stuck-like-Velcro parent could finally let go. There can be no more sticking if one parent can let go. Linda could see that she needed to chart her own course and allow herself to be realistic about what she needed and what Doug could really give her. She decided to give up the dance of hope and abandonment, to give up her part, at least. However, these two keep putting their family together in creative and useful ways.

Everything's working out fine now. It's been over 10 years since that awful Christmas party. I feel very blessed that it has ended this way, because I look around and I see people who are still angry, and I think what a waste of your life to still be so angry.

People look at me oddly, that we get together and talk on the phone. Our kids love to hear us reminisce. Now, I don't hate him in any way. We'll continue to be very good friends. He doesn't have any other family. They're all gone. We've known each other so long. I mean, how many people do you know for that long? I'll never have 40 years with anyone else.

Now, we're best of friends. We celebrate Christmas with the whole family. He's married again. His new wife comes, too, because my son insisted on having all parents present. That was the turning point. Certainly, it was a little bit awkward at first, but now we all get along fine.

Friends often ask me if we'll get back together again one day. I say, "No, we're very good friends. I care about him, but I couldn't live like that anymore." He can reminisce about the past or dream about the future. We could spend hours at that. But, he screwed it up in the present. All the time. (married 1964, separated 1986, divorced 1990, interviewed 2007)

GRANDCHILDREN

When the next generation comes along, some separated parents think about past decisions. The birth may open longings to have a single place for everyone to come to.

I was kind of high on that first Thanksgiving together in 15 years. I hope we do it again, but maybe the kids will start to go to in-laws and splinter a bit in the future. I'm curious to see what will happen when we get to the grandchildren level. It would be nice to have everyone come to one place. (married 1978, separated 1988, divorced 1996, interviewed 2008)

This family came together after 15 years, and this separated father wishes for more. Many separated parents have years of distance and hostility and then change at the birth of a grandchild. A fantasy of togetherness as a family is not a fantasy of reunion as a couple.

When our first grandchild was born, I decided to drop the anger. We both went to the naming service. My behavior is really a modeling for my former husband, spurred on partly by my jealousy and competitiveness. He married a woman who also has children, and she is more balanced about parenting. I wanted more of that for the baby. (married 1968, separated 1989, divorced 1990, interviewed 2007)

Betty had new openness to connection with her former partner after the first grandchild. She saw her own behavior differently and "dropped the anger." And she was able to be honest about the motivation. Competitiveness with her former husband's new wife made it possible to find the benign space for this baby. The effect is letting go of the old angers and hurts. Helpful to everyone.

Many of us have fond memories of going to our own grandparents' houses. Not everyone has fond memories, but, for those of us who do, it is deeply disappointing to not be able to give that to our kids and grandkids. We are all kin when the babies arrive. Use of the term "kin" is especially important in helping children understand the rich connections in their families. We need to normalize these real connections between separated parents. A notion of kinship keeps children at the center, allowing everyone to keep connections and to talk and think about success rather than failure—to support transitions, not division. It is, in part, for grandchildren that I propose the new language of untangling, rearranging, and kinship.

But, there is no guarantee that a baby will change the adult relationships in any particular way. We can only be open to the possibility.

In the next 10 years, I foresee that there's going to be some complication. There'll be grandchildren. How will they move between us? If we can celebrate things together, it will be great. Will everybody be invited to be together? I think those are big questions. I can't predict. I see that as sort of the biggest issue. How the holidays will flow when there are grandchildren. My sense is that they'll invite everybody, and everybody will make their own decisions. But there is tension now with the wedding, so I don't know. We met all together several times at my son's house to do the wedding plans. So it's not that it hasn't happened.

We'll have to see what's next. (married 1970, separated 1985, divorced 1988, interviewed 2008)

WITHHOLDING KINSHIP POSSIBILITIES

Sometimes, one parent or another actively prevents connections. During many of the years of Scott and Abby's separation, Scott's new partner was not allowed to be in the same space with the couple. Abby kept holding on to the possibility of the old partnership—long after the family history moved along a very different path. Scott was in a new committed relationship, but Abby kept insisting on keeping Scott's new partner completely out of the family kinship circle. Scott pounded the table:

These were Abby's orders! She would sit with me at the concerts and graduations, but not if Pam were there. She'd be nice to Pam on the phone, but she didn't want to be seen as this extended stepfamily in public. I think she was holding out for reconciliation. Finally, I had a long talk with Abby and explained that it wasn't Pam's fault that I didn't want to reconcile. Abby wanted to look like an intact family and didn't want to give up her idea of getting back together. She came to terms with it by the time our son graduated from high school.

Everything changed for this family when Abby found a new relationship and married. Scott and Pam were invited to the party the night before Abby's wedding. Their daughter was astounded that her mother and stepmother were in the same room. Their reconnection had been going on for a long time, but their daughter, a college student, hadn't been home to witness the new connections. She knew only the tensions and her mother's refusal to be together in private or public. Big fissures in this family were healed by being in the same place for celebration. This young woman could claim her whole family again.

And recently, when our middle daughter got her master's degree, we all sat together at the graduation and went out for dinner. Our daughter really enjoyed saying, "Here's my mom and stepdad, and here's my dad and stepmom." She was really happy. (married 1978, separated 1988, divorced 1996, interviewed 2008)

IN THE BLOOD

Memories are often carried in our bodies. There are powerful body memories about the long-ago connections. Taking care of babies and young children is loaded with body connections. These parents were former lovers and caregivers of babies and growing kids for many years. The memories run deep, consciously and unconsciously.

> A year or so ago, my daughter called me up and said, all worried, "Oh, Poppy has some trouble with his liver." And it went right through me, and I realized I don't want anything to happen to him. Then I thought—wow—where did that come from? Even today, he's probably in my dreams every night. Somehow, he's there. It's like he's in my blood. I can't get him out. (married 1969, separated 1992, divorced 2000, interviewed 2006)

NO NEW PARTNERS FOR EITHER PARENT

When separated parents have no new partners, there are interesting questions. John and Kate had a hostile history. They had struggled with poverty, and it was a big player in their separation. There had been no contact for years until they both traveled across the country to their son's wedding.

> There was a wedding rehearsal. I was looking around and wondered who this elderly gentleman was, and it was John. They put us together at the wedding, and that was fine. I felt sorry for him because of who he seems to be. He's not a very strong person. He's not one I'd want to spend very much time with. But he has not remarried, and I have not. That is something I think about. I wouldn't get back together, but it's a curiosity. Who we each might have been if circumstances were other. Poverty is just horrific. Poverty really broke us apart. (married 1965, separated 1976, divorced 1978, interviewed 2007)

AGING AND ILLNESS

Throughout the stories, there are references to aging, watching children care for a former partner, thinking of being alone. After a difficult separation and hostility for many years, Leila and her former husband have learned a lot about how to work together. Her former husband's disability had been a difficult part of deciding to separate. She had been his primary caregiver.

> I used to have this nightmare that he would end up on my doorstep when he was old, and I would have to take care of him again. This is funny, because when I think of all we've been through as separated parents, now it would be okay with me to take him in if he was alone. (married 1963, separated 1978, divorced 1980, interviewed 2007)

Several years ago, a story floated about that perhaps was an urban legend, as I could find no references to support it. However, it might make sense. Here it is. Several adult children were suddenly faced with caring for their long-separated parents. Each parent had been diagnosed with Alzheimer's, fairly advanced, and could no longer live alone. The long-ago divorce was full of hostility and tension, and the heat had not subsided over many years. The kids were under pressure to find a place for both parents. Without a lot of resources, they decided to try caring for them in the same house. The parents had not seen each other in many years. It worked. Apparently, they found each other completely charming, no longer able to remember a moment of their turbulent history.

GOODBYES AND RESPECT FOR SEPARATION AND KINSHIP

Of all the people I interviewed, only one had actually faced the death of a former partner. Her story is in chapter 7. In my work setting, however, I heard this touching story from the daughter of parents who had married in the '60s, had two children, divorced, remarried again in the '90s, and divorced again. A total of 33 years married to each other in two separate marriages. And a total of 14 years apart. Their daughter speaks.

> My dad was in the hospital for brain cancer. For the first few days, he was chatty. Each day, he would withdraw a little more. An old family friend wanted my Mom to come to the hospital to say goodbye. I kept thinking about that, but my Dad had been remarried for five years and his wife was very protective and private. Dad's friend insisted, and when he called my Dad's wife, she told him she had been thinking the same thing.
>
> So I called her, and my Mom got down to the hospital in about 20 minutes. She had on this beautiful bright pink blouse, which was not what she usually wore. She wore more the earth tones, neutral, sand colors. Growing up, I always remembered my Dad saying he loved her in bright colors. So I know she thought about him when she put that blouse on.
>
> I was in the room, and she was out in the hallway and I said, "Dad, Mom's here. Can she come in and say hello?" In his deep, deep voice, he said, "Hey, Girl." And he hadn't spoken in days. She asked him if she could sit on the side of his bed. She was holding his hand. She was talking real softly, and he started to cry. My sister and I were in the hallway, and we could see her wipe away his tear. He just lit up.
>
> It was a very short visit. Mom said, "It was the best three minutes I've spent with him in 23 years. I knew I was going to get in there. I didn't know how. I visualized popping out of a laundry cart."

The daughter sighs and remembers.

> This moment was so wonderful, that it got to happen. It was such a gift to me and my sister. We needed to know that they did truly love each other after all the ups and downs of our family life.

He went to hospice the next day and died a few days later. The sisters were on either side of him, holding his hands when he stopped breathing. They were able to tell their mother of his peaceful death. These moments of coming together are so healing.

10

Wisdom for Separated Parents

Remembering and sharing the stories of their separations was powerful for these men and women. They saw new connections in their histories and found new wisdom. "Nobody had to get divorced except us," said one wise grandmother.

The parents interviewed here were married in the '60s, '70s, and '80s. They made their choices about connection and separation within the social and cultural shifts of the late 20th century, a uniquely interesting time of family change and transition. Our larger society was and is still grappling with definitions of family. As these folks looked back, they gave definition to the ways that parents untangle and rearrange. These parents were our pioneers. They broke new ground and helped forge new ways to be successful parents, apart and still connected. What they shared holds up well as a roadmap for parents I know today.

As the parents spoke, many feelings came up. Even though much time had passed since their struggles about separation. They were curious, relieved, and saddened to see their history from a new perspective.

One woman said, "It was interesting to think though all this again. To go back and revisit this history. It makes me want to write about being married to this man and all the experiences we went through, because it was so rich. We were in each other's lives for 15 years. It would be useful for me to look at how I grew as a person. He met me when I was barely 18, and we split up in my early 30s. Those were my adult formative years."

Another man reflected, "From where it is now, it's kind of nice to talk about. It's mostly good stuff. It was very therapeutic to remember the story, good to talk about it again."

Others found new understandings and wisdom. "I enjoyed talking about myself. I haven't done that for a long time. It's so reassuring to share history and have it validated. To really find out that my history is not odd. Talking put all my thoughts into a perspective." This woman has felt "odd" for too many years. These kinds of families, men and women continuing to be connected as parents, don't have to continue to feel "odd."

When telling the stories, many continue to feel some pain. "I have to tell you, talking about this is still very painful, even after 22 years." One woman summed it up: "It's been very interesting to talk about it. Now I need a good cry and a nap."

There may be surprising feelings for separated parents who are now reading this book. Feelings are likely to come up as they remember their own untangling, their own patterns. I hope that everyone will find ways to talk over the feelings and insights that do come up. And to relish the notion of being one of the pioneers who discovered new family forms in the 20th century.

During each interview, I asked for any specific nuggets of wisdom that parents would like to share. I wondered how these pioneers thought about their choices now that their families had lived on into the 21st century. They are our experts about these changes and transitions. They have had time to reflect on life and marriage and separation and parenting.

> I saw my neighbor divorcing and doing it in an angry way. I didn't want to do that. In urban living in 1981, there were lots of divorces. The culture supported divorce. I was not a weirdo to be a divorced woman. But I did not want to stay angry.

These parents had strong feelings about protecting children from the grown-up problems, especially the angry feelings partners may have about each other. Most of the parents had to struggle with what to say to their children at the time of the separation. Some expressed a lot of anger and sadness in front of their children. Some took the victim role. Some attacked the other partner in ways that left them feeling guilty.

> My advice is that when children are younger, don't knock the other party. I feel guilty about that. (married 1967, separated 1978, divorced 1979, interviewed 2008)

> What I learned was that the biggest mistake to avoid is poisoning offspring. Regardless of the choices you've made in your life—good or bad—do not use your kids. And another thing I learned is that even as a parent, you cannot be responsible for the well-being of your kids. Everyone should have their own individual relationships with each parent. I had to learn how not to take responsibility for their relationship with their father. It was really hard because I was always trying to protect them. (married 1985, separated 1996, divorced 1998, interviewed 2008)

She is very proud to have found a balance, to not feel that she had to be the mediator between her children and their father. She learned to have confidence in herself, in her children, and in her former partner. Families are strongest when individuals have relationships one-to-one, with no one person having the responsibility for holding things together.

> What would I tell young parents today? Go back to when you married this person and see what were the things that you really loved. Tell your children about those things. You can be a part of each other's lives in many different ways. Try to regain a perspective. To look at the big picture. I know a number of families who don't speak to each other. That's really sad. Focus on the joys of the children together. When you get caught up in thinking about the things that you didn't like about the person, figure out what you can tolerate and what you can't, and then remove yourself. I try to be honest with my children and honest with myself and try to leave a healthier legacy. (married 1975, separated 1993, divorced 1997, interviewed 2009)

In many regions of the country, there was a certain permissiveness about divorce and, in other sections, much backlash against divorce. This permission/backlash struggle occupied religious and political leaders and set research careers in motion. Great debates flooded the press and churches and schools.[1] One woman spoke with great feeling about how this filtered down and impacted her family.

> I think the culture had gotten too lenient about divorce and too supportive about personal fulfillment. If divorce hadn't been so easy, we wouldn't have been divorced. My husband was able to leave the family and rationalize that it was fine. Everybody was doing it or had done it. I knew that kids could be really, really hurt by divorce. *He* didn't seem to notice the part about kids being really, really hurt by it. So I wish the culture had not been so laissez-faire. If the culture had held our feet to the fire, it really would have been possible to have done more than we did. He told me later, "I just stonewalled. I just didn't want to do the work to figure it all out. I was mad." I benefited personally by the divorce, but I don't think it would have been wrong to stay. I could have stayed in the relationship for the children. (married 1965, separated 1987, divorced 1990, interviewed 2006)

I think of Maya Angelou's wise words when I hear these stories and think of my own decisions: "I did the best at the time with what I had, but when I had more I did better."

And the debates about divorce and children were embedded in larger transitions, especially for women.[2]

As far as the social context of our lives, I think I was caught in the middle. In college I was caught up with a lot of things—the antiwar movement and early feminism and the civil rights movement. Those were all things that were incredibly meaningful to me. I was into the mind-expanding movement, using drugs as a place of experiencing something different. So on the one hand, I was very influenced by all of that—and on the other hand, there were no real social changes, so I didn't see other options. The opportunities for women hadn't really changed. Women were still teachers and nurses. Fifty percent of the women in the class were married in their senior year or getting married that summer. I opted for the tradition, because I didn't know what else to do. I opted out of fear and felt caught by that. We had no models. I think he felt caught by tradition, too. It was very hard to be a pioneer and forge a different way of living. I think I knew that I wasn't ready for marriage, but I didn't have the courage or encouragement to try any-thing different. I couldn't say to myself, so don't get married, go travel right now, or do something different. No one else could say that to me, either. The world wasn't very accepting of that yet.

There were no models for divorce in my family. I was the first one. My mother was very happily married to my father. Her sibs were all in long-term marriages, too. In my family, women stayed at home and weren't professional at all. They were educated but not professional. I never wanted to stay home and raise children. I wanted to do other things. I was very interested in the world of the mind. I loved learning, and I was a good student. I was always encouraged to use my mind, but I wasn't so encouraged to work or do anything like that.

She found a way to have adventure. Her adventures were relationships.

I just started. I really wanted to do that. That was really the motivating factor in the separation. I was already interested in other relationships. I feel a deep sadness about causing pain and guilt. I feel sadness about the hurt that we both felt. Yet I also feel that I had to do that. In order for me to grow and be the person I am today, I had to go through that. It's a terrible paradox. I wish I had not married so soon. I wish my parents had been less protective. They felt that once I was married, they wouldn't have to worry about me again. I wish that it didn't have to go that way, but I certainly did lots to orchestrate it. It isn't as if it just happened. (married 1970, separated 1985, divorced 1988, interviewed 2008)

Exploring other relationships was not the only adventure open to women at that time. Betsy lived in Cambridge, Massachusetts, which in 1969 was a significant center of the emerging women's movement. All over the city, women were meeting in what were called consciousness-raising groups.[2]

Women were exploring their lives as wives and mothers. They were asking questions of the traditional roles and rules. These questioning women made significant contributions to the social and political changes that erupted in the larger society in the '70s and '80s. It was out of these groups that a groundbreaking book about women's health emerged. *Our Bodies, Ourselves*[3] brought a sense of power to many women. Even though Betsy had an original copy of the book, she was fearful of the independence being suggested by these women's groups.

> Someone asked me to come to one of those consciousness-raising meetings. I was very defensive and very, very scared. That says a lot about why I chose my marriage. I was very, very scared of all these things, including feminism and the independence that would mean. The personality of the man I married was my way of censuring myself. I could shut down. On the outside, the women's movement was alluring to me, but I only got involved in my head. I studied it. (married 1969, separated 1996, divorced 2009, interviewed 2010)

Betsy stayed in her marriage for 27 years, with a long in-house separation. She told me she feared losing her family, because there was so much in the culture about "broken families" and predictions of almost certainly problematic lives for kids of divorced parents.

THE LANGUAGE OF BROKEN

Men and women who did decide to separate walked into their new life under the banner of "broken family" and statistics of failure. Headlines screamed about broken families, children of divorce, and single parenting. Statistics foretold dire outcomes for families of divorce.

Over the years, Doug has agonized over his decision to separate and about the impact on his daughters. He feared that the predictions of dire outcomes might be true and kept his fingers crossed until the girls were well into their own adulthood.

> I'll tell you this: it felt like separating was a selfish gesture. But I remember thinking, this is going to kill me. I'll either have a heart attack living in this relationship or become dysfunctional and depressed. I don't have any terror of being alone. But if I stayed, it would have destroyed me.
>
> I'm constantly concerned about whether I did the right thing by the girls. Perhaps it wasn't the right thing for the girls, but the alternative wasn't the right thing, either. So, I don't come up with any magic answer. I don't think I could have done anything much different. I was not growing in that marriage very much, and I think that I'm a better

person now. That pleases me. I can be of service to my children and I was, in that marriage, very twisted and rigid and frightened. I feel good about who I am to my daughters today. (married 1967, separated 1984, divorced 1985, interviewed 2006)

A different language might have helped balance the fears for this man. The words "untangling" and "rearranging" might have helped him to see how his family would continue, not break.

Another woman looks back on the words around separation and divorce. She, too, would have been helped by this new language of continuing kinship. Thank goodness, she was able to use her experience to see a truth about the value of continuing kinship.

> I hated the whole idea of getting divorced, being a statistic. It seemed just awful to me because I wanted to make the marriage a success. But then once I actually went through the whole process of separating and getting divorced, I looked back on it and said: "Excuse me, but my marriage was not a failure." Would I change anything? Maybe I would have gotten out of the marriage earlier. But I think everything has its time, and I think emotionally I couldn't do it until I actually did it. For whatever reason, I don't have any regrets. I don't look back and think I shouldn't have married. We did a lot of great things, and he introduced me to a whole new culture, a whole new language, and I got to live in another country for a year and a half. So we weren't broken. We changed. (married 1969, separated 1992, divorced 2000, interviewed 2006)

STATISTICS

Collecting data on separation is very difficult. "The collection and publication of detailed marriage and divorce statistics was suspended beginning January 1996," announced the U.S. government.[4] Survey forms have no box to check for "continuing to parent." The focus of much research is on the adult relationships that "break," rather than on the continuing kinship of parents around children.

An interesting aspect of the interviews in this book is that most of these parents would have been counted in statistics as single parents. But most were not parenting alone. None was actually a single parent in the way the media and researchers have so popularly defined the term.

For some, there was no clear-cut way to even use the old language. Some parents are missing from the statistics because they "stayed together for the children," while they, as parents, actually lived a very formal separation. Here is Betsy again. She makes it clear that the in-house separation had an impact on her children. But these children were never labeled "children of divorce."

> My kids were children of a very quiet, unlively household, *not* children of divorce. We stayed in the same house until they were in their 20s. My husband and I had very separate lives. My kids had a family model of simmering anger, not custody and visitation arrangements. (married 1969, separated 1996, divorced 2009, interviewed 2010)

How do we classify this family? "Intact?" "Separated?" It is an interesting question, especially to the now-adult children trying to find ways to understand their histories. "Intact," "separated," and "divorced" are words that convey only a very limited understanding of any family.

It will be more difficult for all of us to look at families in more nuanced ways. Changing the language will help. The word "kinship" keeps children in the center of the circle. "Untangling" and "rearranging" are words that make more sense. We can stop the negative language and really look at what is happening for adults and children. This new language is more helpful and gives more creativity back to parents and children, to the extended family, to the next generation. It is also more accurate.

THE CONNECTION OF HISTORY

Why stay in touch with a former partner? One interesting reason given by several interviewees was that their partner had known their parents. That meant a lot. However you feel about your parents, they are not the same when they have aged. No one can complain about them—or recall them lovingly—with as much accuracy as a sibling or a former partner.

Former partners are holders of history and memories about lost children, too, history to be shared and tended.

> Whenever I'm in New England, I call him and we have coffee. But we're not friends. He isn't like a friend I'd call if I needed to talk about something. I care about him, and I know he cares about me. The only reason for the connection is our daughter who died 20 years ago. I've moved a lot, and no one else knows that I was the mother of a daughter, that she died. I mean they know the fact, but they didn't know her, and it doesn't mean anything to them. It has been precious to keep the contact with my daughter's father. My family loves him. His whole family is gone. It's very special that my family does care about him a lot. He came for my mother's 103rd birthday. I was very happy that he did that. My mother hugged him at the party. That was a big surprise. She doesn't hug many people. (married 1954, separated 1979, divorced 1982, interviewed 2007)

WE ARE ALL STORIES

Each story is a maze when it is lived and later a roadmap for someone else. Where will our stories take us next? The twisting paths recounted in this book had some dead ends and many detours. But looking back, they are such exquisite mazes.

Sometimes, it's hard to locate just where you are in a maze. It's good to call out and to hear an answering voice.

Notes

CHAPTER 1

1. Collins, G. (2009). *When Everything Changed: The Amazing Journey of American Women from 1960 to the Present*. New York: Little, Brown.

2. Bridges, W. (2004). *Transitions: Making Sense of Life's Changes*. Cambridge, MA: Da Capo Press.

3. The divorce experience: a study of divorce at midlife and beyond. (2004). Survey conducted by Knowledge Networks, Inc., for AARP.

4. Ahrons, C. (2004). *We're Still Family: What Grown Children Have to Say about Their Parents' Divorce*. New York: HarperCollins.

5. Beal, E. W., & Hockman, G. (1991). *Adult Children of Divorce: Breaking the Cycle and Achieving Success in Love, Marriage and Family*. New York: Delacorte.

6. Berman, C. (1991). *Adult Children of Divorce Speak Out: About Growing up with and Moving beyond Parental Divorce*. New York: Simon & Schuster.

7. Burt, A., Ed. (2006). *My Mother Married Your Father: Writers Talk about Stepparents, Stepchildren, and Everyone in Between*. New York: Norton.

8. Kressell, K., & Deutsch, M. (1977). Divorce therapy: an in-depth survey of therapists' views. *Family Process*, 16, Issue 4 (December), 413.

9. *Los Angeles Times*. (2009). Obituary of James Cook. March 18, p. 4.

10. Robboy, A. W. (2002). *Aftermarriage: The Myth of Divorce: Unspoken Marriage Agreements and Their Impact on Divorce*. Indianapolis: Alpha Books.

11. Coontz, S. (1997). *The Way We Really Are: Coming to Terms with America's Changing Families*. New York: Basic Books.

CHAPTER 2

1. Coontz, S. (1992). *The Way We Never Were: American Families and the Nostalgia Trap*. New York: Basic Books.

2. Ms. magazine first published as insert to *New York* magazine in 1971. Its first stand-alone issue appeared in January 1972.

3. Collins, G. (2009). *When Everything Changed: The Amazing Journey of American Women from 1960 to the Present*. New York: Little, Brown.

4. Friedan, B. (1963). *The Feminine Mystique*. New York: Dell.

CHAPTER 3

1. Schulman, B. J. (2001). *The Seventies: The Great Shift in American Culture, Society, and Politics*. New York: Free Press.

2. Hendrix, H. (2008). *Getting the Love You Want: A Guide for Couples*, 25th Anniversary Ed. New York: Holt Paperbacks.

3. *Statistical Abstract of the United States: 2010, 129th Ed.* (2010). Washington, DC: U.S. Government Printing Office, p. 64.

4. Collins, G. (2009). *When Everything Changed: The Amazing Journey of American Women from 1960 to the Present*. New York: Little, Brown.

5. Rimmer, R. H. (1990). *The Harrad Experiment*, 2nd ed. Amherst, NY: Prometheus.

6 Bridges, W. (2004). *Transitions: Making Sense of Life's Changes*. Cambridge, MA: Da Capo Press.

CHAPTER 4

1. Collins, G. (2009). *When Everything Changed: The Amazing Journey of American Women from 1960 to the Present*. New York: Little, Brown.

2. Brokaw, T. (2007). *Boom! Voices of the Sixties: Personal Reflections on the '60s and Today*. New York: Random House.

3. Ahrons, C. (2004). *We're Still Family: What Grown Children Have to Say about Their Parents' Divorce*. New York: HarperCollins.

4. Weiss, R. S. (1973). *Loneliness: The Experience of Emotional and Social Isolation*. Cambridge, MA: MIT Press.

5. Osborne, J. (1983). *Stepfamilies: The Restructuring Process*. Brookline, MA: EmiJo Publications.

6. Cherlin, A. J. (2009). *The Marriage-Go-Round: The State of Marriage and the Family in America Today*. New York: Knopf.

7. *Los Angeles Times*. (2009). Obituary of James Cook. March 18, p. 4.

8. See www.stepfamilyboston.com (accessed 10/31/10).

9. See Osborne, front cover.

10. Imber-Black, E., Roberts, J., & Whiting, R. A. (2003). *Rituals in Families & Family Therapy, Revised Ed.*, New York: Norton.

11. Coontz, S. (1997). *The Way We Really Are: Coming to Terms with America's Changing Families*. New York: Basic Books.

CHAPTER 5

1. Aslanian, S. (2010). What the divorce revolution has meant for kids. National Public Radio, Weekend Edition Sunday, January 3. www.npr.org/templates/story/story.php?storyId=122127796 (accessed 10/31/10).

2. Lowrance, M. F. (2010). *The Good Karma Divorce: Avoid Litigation, Turn Negative Emotions into Positive Actions, and Get on with the Rest of Your Life*. New York: HarperOne.

3. Burge, K. (2006). Grief over war loss deepens wounds of divorce: estranged parents often at odds on how to remember slain children. *Boston Globe*, April 3, p. B1.

4. Osborne, J. (1999). *My Teacher Said Goodbye Today: Planning for the End of the School Year, 2nd Ed*. Brookline, MA: EmiJo Publications.

5. Osborne, J. (1983). *Stepfamilies: The Restructuring Process*. Brookline, MA: EmiJo Publications.

6. Papernow, P. L. (1993) *Becoming a Stepfamily: Patterns of Development in Remarried Families*. New York: Jossey-Bass.

7. Kressell, K., & Deutsch, M. (1977). Divorce therapy: an in-depth survey of therapists' views. *Family Process*, 16, Issue 4 (December), 413.

8. Coontz, S. (1997). *The Way We Really Are: Coming to Terms with America's Changing Families*. New York: Basic Books.

9. Ricci, I. (1980). *Mom's House, Dad's House: Making Shared Custody Work, How Parents Can Make Two Homes for Their Children after Divorce*. New York: Macmillan.

CHAPTER 7

1. Osborne, J. (1983). *Stepfamilies: The Restructuring Process*. Brookline, MA: EmiJo Publications.

2. Coontz, S. (1997). *The Way We Really Are: Coming to Terms with America's Changing Families*. New York: Basic Books.

3. Collins, G. (2009). *When Everything Changed: The Amazing Journey of American Women from 1960 to the Present*. New York: Little, Brown.

4. Ricci, I. (1980). *Mom's House, Dad's House: Making Shared Custody Work, How Parents Can Make Two Homes for Their Children after Divorce*. New York: Macmillan.

5. Robboy, A. W. (2002). *Aftermarriage: The Myth of Divorce: Unspoken Marriage Agreements and Their Impact on Divorce*. Indianapolis: Alpha Books.

6. Blau, M. (1993). *Families Apart: Ten Keys to Successful Co-Parenting*. New York: A Perigree Book.

7. Kressell, K., & Deutsch, M. (1977). Divorce therapy: an in-depth survey of therapists' views. *Family Process*, 16, Issue 4 (December), 413.

8. Coontz, S. (1992). *The Way We Never Were: American Families and the Nostalgia Trap*. New York: Basic Books.

9. Papernow, P. L. (1993). *Becoming a Stepfamily: Patterns of Development in Remarried Families*. New York: Jossey-Bass.

CHAPTER 8

1. Mosher, W. D., Chandra, A., & Jones J. (2005). Sexual behavior and selected health measures: Men and women 15–44 years of age, United States, 2002. Advance data from vital and health statistics No. 362. Hyattsville, MD: National Center for Health Statistics.

2. See www.familyequality.org/site/PageServer (accessed 10/31/10).

3. Schulenburg, J. (1985). *Gay Parenting: A Complete Guide for Gay Men and Lesbians with Children*. New York: Anchor Press/Doubleday.

4. Coontz, S. (1997). *The Way We Really Are: Coming to Terms with America's Changing Families*. New York: Basic Books.

5. Coontz, S. (1992). *The Way We Never Were: American Families and the Nostalgia Trap*. New York: Basic Books.

6. Altman, D. (1982). *The Homosexualization of America, the Americanization of the Homosexual*. New York: St. Martin's Press.

7. *Los Angeles Times*. (2009). Obituary of James Cook. March 18, p. 4.

8. D'Emillio, J. (1983). *Sexual Politics, Sexual Communities: The Making of a Homosexual Minority in the United States, 1940–1970*. Chicago: University of Chicago Press.

9. Ricci, I. (1980). *Mom's House, Dad's House: Making Shared Custody Work, How Parents Can Make Two Homes for Their Children sfter Divorce*. New York: Macmillan.

10. See www.gaybidads.org (accessed 2/25/11).

11. See www.straightspouse.org (accessed 2/25/11).

12. See www.colage.org (accessed 2/25/11).

CHAPTER 9

1. Collins, G. (2009). *When Everything Changed: The Amazing Journey of American Women from 1960 to the Present*. New York: Little, Brown.

2. See www.patriotledger.com/lifestyle/50_plus/x317593532/IN-SICKNESS-AND-IN-HEALTH-Divorced-Hull-couple-remarries-10-years-after-lifesaving-transplant (accessed 2/25/11).

CHAPTER 10

1. Coontz, S. (1997). *The Way We Really Are: Coming to Terms with America's Changing Families*. New York: Basic Books.

2. Collins, G. (2009). *When Everything Changed: The Amazing Journey of American Women from 1960 to the Present*. New York: Little, Brown.

3. Boston Women's Health Book Collective, Ed. (1976). *Our Bodies, Ourselves: A Book by and for Women*, 2nd ed. New York: Touchstone Books.

4. *Statistical Abstract of the United States: 2010, 129th Ed.* (2010). Washington, DC: U.S. Government Printing Office, p. 64.

Bibliography

Ahrons, C. (2004). *We're Still Family: What Grown Children Have to Say about Their Parents' Divorce*. New York: HarperCollins.

Altman, D. (1982). *The Homosexualization of America, The Americanization of the Homosexual*. New York: St. Martin's Press.

Beal, E. W., & Hockman, G. (1991). *Adult Children of Divorce: Breaking the Cycle and Achieving Success in Love, Marriage and Family*. New York: Delacorte Press.

Berman, C. (1991). *Adult Children of Divorce Speak Out: About Growing up with and Moving beyond Parental Divorce*. New York: Simon & Schuster.

Blau, M. (1993). *Families Apart: Ten Keys to Successful Co-Parenting*. New York: Perigree.

Bridges, W. (2004). *Transitions: Making Sense of Life's Changes*. Cambridge, MA: Da Capo Press.

Brokaw, T. (2007). *Boom! Voices of the Sixties: Personal Reflections on the '60s and Today*. New York: Random House.

Burt, A., Ed. (2006). *My Mother Married Your Father: Writers Talk about Stepparents, Stepchildren, and Everyone in Between*. New York: Norton.

Cherlin, A. J. (2009). *The Marriage-Go-Round: The State of Marriage and the Family in America Today*. New York: Knopf.

Collins, G. (2009). *When Everything Changed: The Amazing Journey of American Women from 1960 to the Present*. New York: Little, Brown.

Coontz, S. (1992). *The Way We Never Were: American Families and the Nostalgia Trap*. New York: Basic Books.

Coontz, S. (1997). *The Way We Really Are: Coming to Terms with America's Changing Families*. New York: Basic Books.

D'Emillio, J. (1983). *Sexual Politics, Sexual Communities: The Making of a Homosexual Minority in the United States, 1940–1970*. Chicago: University of Chicago Press.

Hendrix, H. (2008). *Getting the Love You Want: A Guide for Couples, 25th Anniversary Ed.* New York: Holt Paperbacks.

Osborne, J. (1983). *Stepfamilies: The Restructuring Process*. Brookline, MA: EmiJo Publications.

Papernow, P. L. (1993). *Becoming a Stepfamily: Patterns of Development in Remarried Families*. New York: Jossey-Bass.

Ricci, I. (1980). *Mom's House, Dad's House: Making Shared Custody Work, How Parents Can Make Two Homes for Their Children after Divorce*. New York: Macmillan.

Robboy, A. W. (2002). *Aftermarriage: The Myth of Divorce: Unspoken Marriage Agreements and Their Impact on Divorce*. Indianapolis: Alpha Books.

Schulenburg, J. (1985). *Gay Parenting: A Complete Guide for Gay Men and Lesbians with Children*. New York: Anchor Press/Doubleday.

Schulman, B. J. (2001). *The Seventies: The Great Shift in American Culture, Society, and Politics*. New York: Free Press.

Weiss, R. S. (1973). *Loneliness: The Experience of Emotional and Social Isolation*. Cambridge, MA: MIT Press.

Index

About the Author

JUDY OSBORNE is a marriage and family therapist in Brookline, Massachusetts, and Director of Stepfamily Associates, an organization she founded in 1981. She consults with individuals, couples, and families about the issues of living in stepfamilies (www.stepfamilyboston.com) and has seen, firsthand, the evolution of many postmarriage relationships.

Osborne has always been on the leading edge of new services to families. In 1966, she became the first elementary guidance counselor in the Brookline, Massachusetts, public schools. The establishment of Stepfamily Associates (1981) was an early entry into services for the then-growing numbers of step-families created as the divorce wave reached its peak. In the early 1980s, well before national legislation made hospice services common, she became a founder of a community hospice that served as a model for services to families facing terminal illness. In the early 1990s, she helped create services for adult children of alcoholics, extending family alcoholism services at McLean Hospital in Belmont, Massachusetts.

After graduating from Mount Holyoke College, Osborne studied Child Development at Pacific Oaks College and Children's School. She has advanced degrees in Counseling Psychology from Teachers College, Columbia University, and Northeastern University. In addition, she has a certificate of advanced study from The Boston Institute for Psychotherapy.

Judy grew up in a small town in Connecticut. Her early years were formed with the expectation of lifelong connections to family and community. Cultural changes of the mid-20th century, her own story, and her solid foundation as a family therapist allow her to take a very long view of family change. Her far-flung family includes a daughter and son, a son-in-law, a daughter-in-law, four grandsons, two stepdaughters, and two step-granddaughters, plus the extended family members connected with each one of them. Her former husband and his wife and families complete the kinship circle. These lifelong connections are renewed annually on Cape Cod, where her kids and stepkids played by the sea 40 years ago.